KEPT FOR THE
Master's Use

FRANCES HAVERGAL
DEVOTIONAL ADAPTED BY
KATIE GARRAWAY

Kept For the Master's Use

Remnant Publishing
Copyright © 2024 Caleb & Katie Garraway
ISBN: 979-8-9874913-0-0

REMNANT MINISTRIES
215 S. Marion Avenue
Washington, IA 52353

Remnant Ministries is a ministry sent out of the Marion Avenue Baptist Church. It is our passion that God would use our ministry to reignite a sacred fire in the hearts of His people to unashamedly stand firm and uncompromisingly stay faithful to God's Word. The Lord has never needed a majority to make a difference. We believe that from the youngest to the oldest, it is our time to claim the promises of God and cling to the presence of God and behold what He will do in our generation! **Remnant Ministries** is God-and-Country in nature with a strong three-fold thrust: Redemption to the lost, Revival to the church, and Restoration to the country.

www.remnantministriesonline.com
calebgarraway@gmail.com
917.412.0059

Scripture quotations are from the Authorized King James Version.

All rights reserved. No part of this publication may be reproduced, stored in a retrieval system, or transmitted in any form or by any means — electronic, mechanical, photocopy, recording, or any other — except for brief quotations in printed reviews, without the prior permission of Remnant Ministries and/or Caleb & Katie Garraway.

TABLE OF CONTENTS

Introduction..4
Our Lives Kept for Jesus...10
Our Moments Kept for Jesus...................................27
Our Hands Kept for Jesus..35
Our Feet Kept for Jesus..47
Our Voices Kept for Jesus..53
Our Lips Kept for Jesus..68
Our Silver & Gold Kept for Jesus...........................81
Our Intellects Kept for Jesus...................................94
Our Wills Kept for Jesus..100
Our Hearts Kept for Jesus.....................................107
Our Love Kept for Jesus..113
Our Selves Kept for Jesus......................................119
Christ for Us..128
Conclusion...139
About the Compiler..141

INTRODUCTION
— *by Katie Garraway* —

Frances Ridley Havergal was born in Astley, Worcestershire, England, on December 14, 1836, as the youngest of six children. Her father was a faithful pastor loved by his congregation and community and was described as one who *"takes a text, picks it all to pieces, and shows us what is inside it, and then makes us feel it."*

Frances learned to read by the age of three and even began picking up other languages simply by listening to the tutors teaching her five siblings. By the time she was nine she was helping teach a Sunday school class for younger children.

However, Frances's life took a poignant turn when her mother passed away in 1848, leaving a void in her heart at the tender age of twelve. Two years later, she was sent to a private school for girls in London to help her in her further studies. It was during this time that she came face-to-face with her personal need for the Saviour. Soon after her fifteenth birthday, she joyfully accepted the Lord. She wrote: *"I committed my soul to the Saviour . . . and earth and heaven seemed bright from that moment!"*

Devotional Inspired by "Take My Life & Let It Be"

After this, her life blossomed as a gifted young woman. She honed her linguistic skills, learning several languages including German, Hebrew, Greek, Latin, and French. She grew fond of writing poetry and prose. She excelled as a pianist and singer, captivating audiences with her beautiful voice and musical ability. However, she recognized that her gifts were not for herself but were on loan to her by God to serve Him and further the spread of the Gospel.

Frances humbly lived her life with complete dedication to the ministry. As a result of this, God lifted her up and used her as an incredible vessel for His service. Despite facing bouts of physical weakness and failing health, she was known by those who worked with her for being enthusiastic and vigorous in service to others, the lost, and her loving Saviour. She taught Sunday schools and ladies' services, helped conduct religious meetings, and sang and played often for evangelistic crusades.

God used her as a prolific author, writing many pamphlets and books for children and adults alike. In fact, C. H. Spurgeon was so impressed with her work that in 1879 the three hundred pastors who attended his annual conference called "Pastors' College" were given two of her books. He said that they were *"choice and dainty morsels for their spiritual refreshment and quickening."*

But Havergal's greatest gift the composing of timeless hymns. She approached her writing with deep reverence, never composing lyrics without first praying over them. Concerning the creative process, she wrote: *"I can never set myself to write verse. I believe my King suggests a thought and whispers me a musical line or two, and then I look up and thank Him delightedly, and go on with it. That is how the hymns and poems* come. I am always ready to welcome it and work when it comes, but I never press for it. There is silence . . . till he sends it."

She was also committed to making sure that her hymns clearly expressed Biblical truth. In some of the manuscript copies, she even attached a Scripture reference to each line. Many of her hymns are filled with an expression to know Christ more and to serve Him with an ever-increasing passion.

"Take my life and Let It Be" is probably her best-known hymn and is certainly a fitting summary of her testimony. In the lyrics, she committed every aspect of her life to the Lord for His purpose.

"*I went for five days,*" wrote Frances Havergal, explaining what prompted her to write this beloved song during a ministry visit to London. "There were ten persons in the house [where I was staying]; *some were unconverted and long prayed for, some converted but not rejoicing Christians. God gave me the prayer, 'Lord, give me all in this house.' And He did!*"

Before she left, everyone had either gotten saved or became reignited in their walk with God. On the final night of her stay after she had already retired for the evening, the lady who ran the boarding home knocked on her door, apologized for the intrusion, and told her that her two daughters wished to see her. "*They were much troubled over their spiritual condition and were weeping, but I was able to show them the way of Life, and they were both joyfully converted that night! I was too happy to sleep and passed most of the night in renewal of my consecration, and those little couplets formed themselves and chimed in my heart one after another till they finished with 'ever only, ALL FOR THEE!' I saw clearly the blessedness of true consecration. I saw it* as a flash of electric light, and what you see you can never unsee. There must be full surrender before there can be full blessedness!" From its birth in the late-night hours of February 4, 1874, to today, "Take My Life And Let It Be" still speaks to believers around the world. Each line begins with the compulsory verb "Take," giving the sense of a continual prayer of surrender. This is certainly a needed call to each of us that we should embrace personally. Have you consecrated *everything* to God?

These lyrics were not just words on a page to Miss Havergal. They came out of a personal deep-seated conviction that became the standard for her own living. One of the lines of the hymn says, "Take my silver and my gold; not a mite would I withhold." In 1878, four years after writing the hymn, Miss Havergal wrote a friend, "The Lord has shown me another little step, and, of course, I have taken it with extreme delight. 'Take my silver and my gold' now means shipping off all my ornaments to the Church Missionary House, including a jewel cabinet that is really fit for a countess, where all will be accepted and disposed of for me . . . Nearly fifty articles are being packed up. I don't think I ever packed a box with such pleasure."

Though Havergal's health was frail during much of her adult years, she spent her full energy living for Christ. God used her to write 71 hymns in her lifetime, including "I Gave My Life for Thee," "Like a River Glorious," and "Who Is on the Lord's Side?" Frances Havergal's life was a shining example of true consecration and devotion to the Lord. At the young age of 42, she went Home to be with her Saviour.

The diary of her faithful sister, Marie, gives an account of her last sickness (peritonitis) and departure. Her peace and joy shone through all her suffering, while her patience and unselfish consideration for others were most striking. *"June 3rd. There came a terrible rush of convulsive sickness. When it ceased, the nurse gently assisting her, she nestled down in the pillows, folded her hands on her breast, saying: 'There, now it's all over! Blessed rest!' And now she looked up steadfastly as if she saw the Lord, and surely nothing less heavenly could have reflected such a glorious radiance upon her face! For ten minutes we watched that almost visible meeting with her King, and her countenance was so glad, as if she were already talking to Him. Then she tried to sing, but after one sweet high note 'HE—', her voice failed, and as her brother commended her soul into her Redeemer's hand she passed away. Our precious sister was gone, –satisfied, –glorified, –within the palace of her King!"*

This reprint of her final book ever written, published after her death, delves deeper into the heart of Frances Havergal as each chapter focuses on another couplet from her hymn, **"Take My Life and Let It Be"**. Each chapter is a convicting, passionate message from her heart to yours and ends with thought-provoking questions to meditate on that I have added. I pray your heart will be stirred by the message of each line of Havergal's song and convicted as you ponder each question. Are we surrendered? Are we willing to give up anything for our Lord? Prayerfully, by the end of this book, we will be!

Take my life, and let it be
Consecrated, Lord, to Thee.

Take my moments and my days;
Let them flow in ceaseless praise.

Devotional Inspired by "Take My Life & Let It Be"

---

*Take my hands, and let them move
At the impulse of Thy love.*

*Take my feet, and let them be
Swift and "beautiful" for Thee.*

*Take my voice, and let me sing
Always, only, for my King.*

*Take my lips, and let them be
Filled with messages from Thee.*

*Take my silver and my gold;
Not a mite would I withhold.*

*Take my intellect, and use
Every power as Thou shalt choose.*

*Take my will and make it Thine;
It shall be no longer mine.*

*Take my heart; it is Thine own;
It shall be Thy royal throne.*

*Take my love; my Lord, I pour
At Thy feet its treasure-store.*

*Take myself, and I will be
Ever, only, ALL for Thee.*

CHAPTER 1
Our Lives Kept For Jesus

"*Keep my life, and let it be
Consecrated, Lord, to Thee.*"

Many a heart has echoed this little song, and yet those echoes have not been, in every case and at all times, so clear, and full, and firm, so continuously glad as we would wish, and perhaps expected. Some of us have said:

"*I launch me forth upon a sea
Of boundless love and tenderness...*"

And after a little we have found, or fancied, that there is a hidden leak in our boat, and though we are doubtless still afloat, yet we are not sailing with the same free, exultant confidence as at first. What is it that has dulled and weakened the echo of our consecration song? what is the little leak that hinders the swift and buoyant course of our consecrated life? — *Holy Father, let*

Thy loving Spirit guide my hand that writes, and strengthen the heart of every one who reads what shall be written, for Jesus' sake.

While many a sorrowfully-varied answer to these questions may, and probably will, arise from touched and sensitive consciences, each being shown by God's faithful Spirit the special sin, the special yielding to temptation which has hindered and spoiled the blessed life which they sought to enter and enjoy, it seems to me that one or other of two things has lain at the outset of the failure and disappointment.

First, it may have arisen from want of the simplest belief in the simplest fact, as well as want of trust in one of the simplest and plainest words our gracious Master ever uttered! The unbelieved fact being simply that He hears us; the untrusted word being one of those plain, broad foundation-stones on which we rested our whole weight, it may be many years ago, and which we had no idea we ever doubted, or were in any danger of doubting now, — *"Him that cometh to Me I will in no wise cast out."*

"Take my life!" We have said it or sung it before the Lord, it may be many times; but if it were only once whispered in His ear with full purpose of heart, should we not believe that He heard it? And if we know that He heard it, should we not believe that He has answered it, and fulfilled this, our heart's desire? For with Him hearing means heeding. Then why should we doubt that He did verily take our lives when we offered them — our bodies when we presented them? Have we not been wronging His faithfulness all this time by practically, even if unconsciously, doubting whether the prayer ever really reached Him? And if so, is it any wonder that we have not realized all the power and joy of full consecration?

By some means or other He has to teach us to trust implicitly at every step of the way. And so, if we did not really trust in this matter, He has had to let us find out our want of trust by withholding the sensible part of the blessing, and thus stirring us up to find out why it is withheld.

An offered gift must be either accepted or refused. Can He have refused it when He has said, *"Him that cometh to Me I will in no wise cast out"*? If not, then it must have been accepted. It is just the same process as when we came to Him first of all, with the intolerable burden of our sins. There was no help for it but to come with them to Him, and take His word for it that He would not and did not cast us out. And so coming, so believing, we found rest to our souls; we found that His word was true, and that His taking away our sins was a reality.

Some give their lives to Him then and there — and go forth to live thenceforth not at all unto themselves, but unto Him who died for them. This is as it should be, for conversion and consecration ought to be simultaneous. But practically it is not very often so, except with those in whom the bringing out of darkness into marvellous light has been sudden and dazzling, and full of deepest contrasts.

More frequently the work resembles the case of the Hebrew servant described in Exodus 21 — who, after six years' experience of a good master's service, dedicates himself voluntarily, unreservedly, and irrevocably to it, saying, *"I love my master; I will not go out free;"* the master then accepting and sealing him to a life-long service, free in law; yet bound in love. This seems to be a figure of later consecration founded on experience and love.

And yet, as at our first coming, it is less than nothing, worse than nothing that we have to bring; for our lives, even our redeemed and pardoned lives, are not only weak and worthless, but defiled and sinful. But thanks be to God for the Altar that sanctifieth the gift, even our Lord Jesus Christ Himself! By Him we draw nigh unto God; to Him, as one with the Father, we offer our living sacrifice; in Him, as the Beloved of the Father, we know it is accepted.

So, dear friends, when once He has wrought in us the desire to be altogether His own, and put into our hearts the prayer, *"Take my life,"* let us go on our way rejoicing, believing that He has taken our lives, our hands, our feet, our voices, our intellects, our wills, our whole selves, to be ever, only, all for Him. Let us consider that a blessedly settled thing; not because of anything we have felt, or said, or done, but because we know that He heareth us, and because we know that He is true to His word.

But suppose our hearts do not condemn us in this matter, our disappointment may arise from another cause. It may be that we have not received, because we have not asked a fuller and further blessing. Suppose that we did believe, thankfully and surely, that the Lord heard our prayer, and that He did indeed answer and accept us, and set us apart for Himself; and yet we find that our consecration was not merely miserably incomplete, but that we have drifted back again almost to where we were before. Or suppose things are not quite so bad as that, still we have not quite all we expected; and even if we think we can truly say, *"O God, my heart is fixed,"* we find that, to our daily sorrow, somehow or other the details of our conduct do not seem to be fixed, something or other is perpetually slipping through, till we get perplexed and distressed. Then we are tempted to wonder whether after all there was not some mistake about it, and the Lord did not really take us at our word, although we took Him at His word. And the struggle with one doubt, and entanglement, and temptation only seems to land us in another. *What is to be done then?*

I think, very humbly and utterly honestly to search and try our ways before our God; or rather, as we shall soon realize our helplessness to make such a search, ask Him to do it for us, praying for His promised Spirit to show us unmistakably if there is any secret thing with us that is hindering both the inflow and outflow of His grace to us and through us.

Do not let us shrink from some unexpected flash into a dark corner; do not let us wince at the sudden touching of a hidden plague-spot. The Lord always does His own work thoroughly if we will only let Him do it; if we put our case into His hands, He will search and probe fully and firmly, though very tenderly. Very painfully, it may be, but only that He may do the very thing we want — cleanse us and heal us thoroughly, so that we may set off to walk in real newness of life.

But if we do not put it unreservedly into His hands, it will be no use thinking or talking about our lives being consecrated to Him. The heart that is not entrusted to Him for searching, will not be undertaken by Him for cleansing; the life that fears to come to the light lest any deed should be reproved, can never know the blessedness and the privileges of walking in the light.

But what then? When He has graciously again put a new song in our mouth, and we are singing, *"Ransomed, healed, restored, forgiven, who like me His praise should sing?"* And again with fresh earnestness we are saying — *"Take my life, and let it be consecrated, Lord, to Thee!"*

Are we only to look forward to the same disappointing experience over again? Are we always to stand at the threshold? Consecration is not so much a step as a course; not so much an act, as a position to which a course of action inseparably belongs. In so far as it is a course and a position, there must naturally be a definite entrance upon it, and a time, it may be a moment, when that entrance is made. That is when we say, *"Take"*; but we do not want to go on taking a first step over and over again. What we want now is to be maintained in that position, and to fulfil that course. So let us go on to another prayer. Having already said, *"Take my life, for I cannot give it to Thee,"* let us now say, with deepened conviction, that without Christ we really can do nothing — Lord, please — *"Keep my life, for I cannot keep it for Thee."*

Let us ask this with the same simple trust to which, in so many other things, He has so liberally and graciously responded. For this is the confidence that we have in Him, that if we ask anything according to His will, He heareth us; and if we know that He hears us, whatsoever we ask, we know that we have the petitions that we desired of Him. There can be no doubt that this petition is according to His will because it is based upon many a promise. May I give it you just as it floats through my own mind again and again, knowing whom I have believed, and being persuaded that He is *able to keep* that which I have committed unto Him?

> **TAKE** my life, and let it be
> Consecrated, Lord, to Thee ... **NOW** —

Keep my moments and my days;
Let them flow in ceaseless praise.

Keep my hands, and they may move
At the impulse of Thy love.

Keep my feet, and they may be
Swift and "beautiful" for Thee.

Keep my voice, that I may sing
Always, only, for my King.

Keep my lips, that they may be
Filled with messages from Thee.

Keep my silver and my gold;
Not a mite would I withhold.

Keep my intellect and use
Every power as Thou shalt choose.

Keep my will, oh *keep* it Thine;
For it is no longer mine.

Keep my heart; it *is* Thine!
It is now Thy royal throne.

Keep my love; my Lord, I pour
At Thy feet its treasure-store.

Keep myself, that I will be
Ever, *only*, ALL for Thee.

Yes! He who is able and willing to take unto Himself, is no less able and willing to keep for Himself. Our willing offering has been made by His enabling grace, and this our King has *"seen with joy."* And now we pray, *"Keep this forever in the imagination of the thoughts of the heart of Thy people"* (I Chronicles 29:17-18). This blessed *"taking,"* once for all, which we may quietly believe as an accomplished fact, followed by the continual *"keeping,"* for which He will be continually inquired of by us, seems analogous to the great washing by which we have part in Christ, and the repeated washing of the feet for which we need to be continually coming to Him. For with the deepest and sweetest consciousness that He has indeed taken our lives to be His very own, the need of His active and actual keeping of them in every detail and at every moment is most fully realized.

But then we have the promise of our faithful God, *"I the Lord do keep it, I will keep it night and day."* The only question is, will we trust this promise, or will we not? If we do, we shall find it come true. If not, of course it will not be realized. For unclaimed promises are like uncashed cheques; they will keep us from bankruptcy, but not from want But if not, *why* not? What right have we to pick out one of His faithful sayings, and say we don't expect Him to fulfil that? What defense can we bring, what excuse can we invent, for so doing?

If you appeal to experience against His faithfulness to His word, I will appeal to experience too, and ask you, did you ever realty trust Jesus to fulfil any word of His to you, and find your

17

trust deceived? As to the past experience of the details of your life not being kept for Jesus, look a little more closely at it, and you will find that though you may have asked, you did not trust Whatever you did really trust Him to keep, He has kept, and the unkept things were never really entrusted. Scrutinize this past experience as you. will, and it will only bear witness against your unfaithfulness, never against His absolute faithfulness.

Yet this witness must not be unheeded. We must not forget the things that are behind till they are confessed and forgiven. Let us now bring all this unsatisfactory past experience, and most of all, the want of trust which has been the poison-spring of its course, to the precious blood of Christ, which cleanseth us, even us, from all sin, even this sin. Perhaps we never saw that we were not trusting Jesus as He deserves to be trusted; if so, let us wonderingly hate ourselves the more that we could be so trustless to such a Saviour, and so sinfully dark and stupid that we did not even see it. And oh, let us wonderingly love Him the more that He has been so patient and gentle with us, upbraiding not, though in our slow-hearted foolishness we have been grieving Him by this subtle unbelief; and then, by His grace, may we enter upon a new era of experience, our lives kept for Him more fully than ever before, because we trust Him more simply and unreservedly to keep them!

Here we must face a question, and perhaps a difficulty. Does it not almost seem as if we were at this point led to trusting to our trust, making everything hinge upon it, and thereby only removing a subtle dependence upon ourselves one step farther back, disguising instead of renouncing it? If Christ's keeping depends upon our trusting, and our continuing to trust depends upon ourselves, we are in no better or safer position than before, and shall only be landed in a fresh series of disappointments. The old story, something. for the sinner to do, crops up again here, only with the ground shifted from *"works"* to trust.

Said a friend to me, *"I see now! I did trust Jesus to do everything else for me, but I thought that this trusting was something that I had got to do."* And so, of course, what she *"had got to do"* had been a perpetual effort and frequent. failure. We can no more trust and keep on trusting than we can do anything else of ourselves. Even in this it must be *"Jesus only"*; we are not to look to Him only to be the Author and Finisher of our faith, but we are to look to Him for all the intermediate fulfilment of the work of faith (II Thessalonians 1:2); we must ask Him to go on fulfilling it in us, committing even this to His power.

For we both may and must
Commit our very faith to Him,
Entrust to Him our trust.

What a long time it takes us to come down to the conviction, and still more to the realization of the fact that without Him we can do *nothing*, but that He must work *all* our work in us! This is the work of God, that ye believe. in Him whom He has sent And no less must it be the work of God that we go on believing, and that we go on trusting. Then, dear friends, who are longing to trust Him with unbroken and unwavering trust, cease the effort and drop the burden, and *now* entrust your trust to Him! He is just as well able to keep that as any other part of the complex lives which we want Him to take and keep for Himself. And oh, do not pass on content with the thought, *"Yes, that is a good idea; perhaps I should find that a great help!"* But, *"Now, then, do it."* It is no help to the sailor to see a flash of light across a dark sea, if he does not instantly steer accordingly.

Consecration is not a religiously selfish thing. If it sinks into that, it ceases to be consecration. We want our lives kept, not that we may feel happy, and be saved the distress consequent on wandering, and get the power with God and man, and all the other privileges linked with it. We shall have all this, because the lower is included in the higher; but our true aim, if the love of Christ constraineth us, will be far beyond this.

Not for *"me"* at all but *"for Jesus"*; not for my safety, but for His glory; not for my comfort, but for His joy; not that I may find rest, but that He may see the travail of His soul, and be satisfied! Yes, for Him *I* want to be kept. Kept for His sake; kept for His use; kept to be His witness; kept for His joy! Kept for Him, that in me He may show forth some tiny sparkle of His light and beauty; kept to do His will and His work in His own way; kept, it may be, to suffer for His sake; kept for Him, that He may do just what seemeth Him good with me; kept, so that no other lord shall have any more dominion over me, but that Jesus shall have all there is to have;—little enough, indeed, but not divided or diminished by any other claim. Is not this, O you who love the Lord — is not this worth living for, worth asking for, worth trusting for?

THIS IS CONSECRATION — and I cannot tell you the blessedness of it. It is not the least use arguing with one who has had but a taste of its blessedness, and saying to him, *"How can these things be?"* It is not the least use starting all sorts of difficulties and theoretical suppositions about it with such a one, any more than it was when the Jews argued with the man who said, *"One thing I know, that whereas I was blind, now I see."* The

Lord Jesus does take the life, that is offered to Him, and He does keep the life for Himself that is entrusted to Him; but until the life is offered we cannot know the taking, and until the life is entrusted we cannot know or understand the keeping. All we can do is to say, *"O taste and see!"* and bear witness to the reality of Jesus Christ, and set to our seal that we have found Him true to His every word, and that we have proved Him able even to do exceeding abundantly above all we asked or thought. Why should we hesitate to bear this testimony?

We have done nothing at all; we have, in all our efforts, only proved to ourselves, and perhaps to others, that we had no power either to give or keep our lives. Why should we not, then, glorify His grace by acknowledging that we have found Him so wonderfully and tenderly gracious and faithful in both taking and keeping as we never supposed or imagined? I shall never forget the smile and emphasis with which a poor working man bore this witness to his Lord. I said to him, *"Well, Brother Henry, we have a good Master, have we not?"*

"Ah," said he, *"a deal better than ever I thought!"*

That summed up his experience, and so it will sum up the experience of every one who will but yield their lives wholly to the same good Master.

I cannot close this chapter without a word with those, especially my younger friends, who, although they have named the name of Christ, are saying, *"Yes, this is all very well for some people, or for older people, but I am not ready for it; I can't say I see my way to this sort of thing."*

I am going to take the lowest ground for a minute, and appeal to *your* "past experience." Are you satisfied with your experience of the other "sort of thing"? Your pleasant pursuits, your harmless recreations, your nice occupations, even your improving ones, what fruit are you having from them? Your social intercourse, your daily talks and walks, your investments of all the time that remains to you over and above the absolute duties God may have given you, what fruit that shall remain have you from all this? Day after day passes on, and year after year, and what shall the harvest be? What is even the present return? Are you getting any real and lasting satisfaction out of it all? Are you not finding that things lose their flavour, and that you are spending your strength day after day for nought? That you are no more satisfied than you were a year ago rather less so, if anything?

Does not a sense of hollowness and weariness come over you as you go on in the same round, perpetually getting through things only to begin again? It cannot be otherwise. Over even the freshest and purest earthly fountains the Hand that never makes a mistake has written, *"He that drinketh of this water shall thirst again."* Look into your own heart and you will find a copy of that inscription already traced, *"Shall thirst again."* And the characters are being deepened with every attempt to quench the inevitable thirst and weariness in life, which can only be satisfied and rested in full consecration to God. For *"Thou hast made us for Thyself, and the heart never resteth till it findeth rest in Thee."* To-day I tell you of a brighter and happier life, whose inscription is, *"Shall never thirst,"* — a life that is no dull round-and-round in a circle of unsatisfactorinesses, but a life that has found its true and entirely satisfactory centre, and set itself towards a shining and entirely satisfactory goal, whose brightness is cast over every step of the way. Will you not seek it?

Do not shrink, and suspect, and hang back from what it may involve, with selfish and unconfiding and ungenerous half-heartedness, Take the word of any who have willingly offered themselves unto the Lord, that the life of consecration is *"a deal better than they thought!"* Choose this day whom you will serve with real, thorough-going, whole-hearted service, and He will receive you; and you will find, as we have found, that He is such a good Master that you are satisfied with His goodness, and that you will never want to go out free. Nay, rather take His own word for it; see what He says: *"If they obey and serve Him, they shall spend their days in prosperity, and their years in pleasures."* You cannot possibly understand that till you are really *in* His service! For He does not give, nor even show, His wages before you enter it And He says, *"My servants shall sing for joy of heart."*

But you cannot try over that song to see what it is like, you cannot even read one bar of it, till your nominal or even promised service is exchanged for real and undivided consecration. But when He can call you *"My servant,"* then you will find yourself singing for joy of heart, because He says you shall.

"And who, then, is willing to consecrate his service this day unto the Lord?"

Do not startle at the term, or think, because you do not understand all it may include, you are therefore not qualified for it. I daresay it comprehends a great deal more than either you or I understand, but we can both enter into the spirit of it, and the detail will unfold itself as long as our probation shall last. Christ demands a hearty consecration in *will*, and He will teach us what that involves in *act*.

This explains the paradox that full consecration may be in one sense the act of a moment, and in another the work of a lifetime. It must be complete to be real, and yet if real, it is always incomplete; a point of rest, and yet a perpetual progression.

Suppose you make over a piece of ground to another person. You give it up, then and there, entirely to that other; it is no longer in your own possession; you no longer dig and sow, plant and reap, at your discretion or for your own profit. His occupation of it is total; no other has any right to an inch of it; it is his affair thenceforth. What crops to arrange for and how to make the most of it but his practical occupation of it may not appear all at once. There may be waste land which he will take into full cultivation only by degrees, space wasted for want of draining or by over fencing, and odd comers lost for want of enclosing; fields yielding smaller returns than they might because of hedgerows too wide and shady, and trees too many and spreading, and strips of good soil trampled into uselessness for want of defined pathways.

Just so is it with our lives. The transaction of, so to speak, making them over to God is definite and complete. But then begins the practical development of consecration. And here He leads on *"softly, according as the children be able to endure."* I do not suppose anyone sees anything like all that it involves at the outset. We have not a notion what an amount of waste of power there has been in our lives; we never measured out the odd comers and the undrained bits, and it never occurred to us what good fruit might be grown in our straggling hedgerows, nor how the shade of our trees has been keeping the sun from the scanty crops.

And so, season by season, we shall be sometimes not a little startled, yet always very glad, as we find that bit by bit the Master shows how much more may be made of our ground, how much more He is able to make of it than we did; and we shall be willing to work under Him and do exactly what He points out, even if it comes to cutting down a shady tree or clearing out a ditch full of pretty weeds and wild-flowers.

As the seasons pass on, it will seem as if there was always more and more to be done; One fact that He is constantly showing us something more to be done in it, proving that it is really His ground. Only let Him have the ground, no matter how poor or overgrown the soil may be, and then *"He will make her wilderness like Eden, and her desert like the garden of the Lord."* Yes, even our *"desert"*! And then we shall sing, *"My beloved is gone down into His garden, to the beds of spices, to feed in the gardens and to gather lilies."*

Made for Thyself, O God!
Made for Thy love, Thy service, Thy delight;
Made to show forth Thy wisdom, grace, and might;
Made for Thy praise, whom veiled archangels laud:
Oh, strange and glorious thought, that we may be
A joy to Thee!

Yet the heart turns away
From this grand destiny of bliss, and deems
'Twas made for its poor self, for passing dreams,
Chasing illusions melting day by day,
Till for ourselves we read on this world's best,
"This is not rest!"

Pondering Points
BY KATIE GARRAWAY

Do you believe that God can use your life in a great way for His glory and the furtherance of the Gospel? Do you truly believe that your life has Divine purpose, and are you yielded to the Lord to reach that potential? Do you remember the time when you surrendered your life completely to Him? Do you find yourself doubting that God has heard your prayer of surrender? Remember His promise in John 6:37, "Him that cometh to Me I will in no wise cast out." Ask God to help you stand in confidence on His promises and take away any doubt that may reside in your heart. "God is faithful, by whom ye were called unto the fellowship of his Son Jesus Christ our Lord." (I Corinthians 1:9).

Many times our sin, flesh and worldliness causes us to slowly take ourselves off of the altar of surrender. Do you feel as if you're always standing at the threshold of full surrender, taking that first step over and over again and therefore never truly experiencing the release, joy and blessings of a surrendered life? Remember that the unfaithfulness is never with God; it always lies with us. Does God truly have all of you? Pray now and yield your life fully over to Him. Then commit to faithfully follow Him and you will see through the years how He faithfully prunes, sows, plants, trims and reveals a beautiful fruit-yielding garden in your life that brings Him great joy and pleasure!

There is nothing more precious than a life that is fully surrendered to God — because this is a life that He will fully use and bless in a great way.

CHAPTER 2
Our Moments Kept For Jesus

*"Keep my moments and my days;
Let them flow in ceaseless praise."*

It will be a help to writer and reader if we consider some of the practical details of the life which we desire to have *"kept for Jesus"* in the order of the little hymn at the beginning of this book, with the one word *"take"* changed to *"keep."* Therefore, we will take a couplet for each chapter.

The first point that naturally comes up is that which is almost synonymous with life — our time. And this brings us at once face to face with one of our past difficulties, and its probable cause.

When we take a wide sweep, we are so apt to be vague. When we are aiming at generalities we do not hit the practicalities. We forget that faithfulness to principle is only proved by faithfulness in detail. Has not this vagueness had something to do with the constant ineffectiveness of our feeble desire that our time should be devoted to God?

In things spiritual, the greater does not always include the less, but, paradoxically, the less more often includes the greater. So in this case, time is entrusted to us to be traded with for our Lord. But we cannot grasp it as a whole. We instinctively break it up ere we can deal with it for any purpose. So when a new year comes round, we commit it with special earnestness to the Lord. But as we do so, are we not conscious of a feeling that even a year is too much for us to deal with? And does not this feeling, that we are dealing with a larger thing than we can grasp, take away from the sense of reality?

Thus, we are brought to a more manageable measure; and as the Sunday mornings or the Monday mornings come round, we thankfully commit the opening week to Him, and the sense of help and rest is renewed and strengthened. But not even the six or seven days are close enough to our hand; even to-morrow exceeds our tiny grasp, and even to-morrow's grace is therefore not given to us. So we find the need of considering our lives as a matter of day by day, and that any more general committal and consecration of our time does not meet the case so truly. Here we have found much comfort and help, and if results have not been entirely satisfactory, they have, at least, been more so than before we reached this point of subdivision.

But if we have found help and blessing by going a certain distance in one direction, is it not probable we shall find more if we go farther in the same? And so, if we may commit the days to our Lord, why not the hours, and why not the moments? And may we not expect a fresh and special blessing in so doing?

We do not realize the importance of moments. Only let us consider those two sayings of God about them, *"In a moment shall they die,"* and, *"We shall all be changed in a moment,"* and we shall think less lightly of them. Eternal issues may hang upon any one of them, but it has come and gone before we can even think about it Nothing seems less within the possibility of our own keeping, yet nothing is more inclusive of all other keeping. Therefore, let us ask Him to keep them for us.

Are they not the tiny joints in the harness through which the darts of temptation pierce us? Only give us time, we think, and we should not be overcome. Only give us time, and we could pray and resist, and the devil would flee from us I But he comes all in a moment; and in a moment—an unguarded, unkept one—we utter the hasty or exaggerated word, or think the un-Christ-like thought, or feel the un-Christlike impatience or resentment.

But even if we have gone so far as to say, *"Take my moments,"* have we gone the step farther, and really *let* Him take them — really entrusted them to Him? It is no good saying *"take"* when we do not let go. How can another keep that which we are keeping hold of? So let us, with full trust in His power, first commit these slippery moments to Him — put them right into His hand — and then we may trustfully and happily say, *"Lord, keep them for me! Keep every one of the quick series as it arises. I cannot keep them for Thee; do Thou keep them for Thyself!"*

But the sanctified and Christ — loving heart cannot be satisfied with only negative keeping. We do not want only to be kept from displeasing Him, but to be kept always pleasing Him. Every *"kept from"* should have its corresponding and still more blessed *"kept for."* We do not want our moments to be simply kept from Satan's use, but kept for His use; we want them to be not only kept from sin, but kept for His praise.

Do you ask, *"But what use can He make of mere moments?"* I will not stay to prove or illustrate the obvious truth that, as are the moments so will be the hours and the days which they build. You understand that well enough. I will answer your question as it stands.

Look back through the history of the Church in all ages, and mark how often a great work and mighty influence grew out of a mere moment in the life of one of God's servants; a mere moment — but overshadowed and filled with the fruitful power of the Spirit of God. The moment may have been spent in uttering five words, but they have fed five thousand, or even five hundred thousand. Or it may have been lit by the flash of a thought that has shone into hearts and homes throughout the land, and kindled torches that have been borne into earth's darkest corners. The rapid speaker or the lonely thinker little guessed what use his Lord was making of that single moment There was no room in it for even a thought of that If that moment had not been, though perhaps unconsciously, *"kept for Jesus,"* but had been otherwise occupied, what a harvest to His praise would have been missed!

The same thing is going on every day. It is generally a moment — either an opening or a culminating one — that really does the work. It is not so often a whole sermon as a single short sentence in it that wings God's arrow to a heart It is seldom a whole conversation that is the means of bringing about the desired result, but some sudden turn of thought or word, which comes with the electric touch of God's power. Sometimes it is less than that; only a look (and what is more momentary?) has been used by Him for the pulling down of strongholds. Again, in our own quiet waiting upon God, as moment after moment glides past in the silence at His feet, the eye resting upon a page of His Word, or only looking up to Him through the darkness, have we not found that He can so irradiate one passing moment with His light that its rays never die away, but shine on and on through days and years? Are not such moments proved to have been kept for Him? And if some, why not all?

This view of moments seems to make it clearer that it is impossible to serve two masters, for it is evident that the service of a moment cannot be divided. If it is occupied in the service of self, or any other master, it is not at the Lord's disposal; He cannot make use of what is already occupied.

Oh, how much we have missed by not placing them at His disposal! What might He not have done with the moments freighted with self or loaded with emptiness, which we have carelessly let drift by! Oh, what might have been if they had all been kept for Jesus! How He might have filled them with His light and life, enriching our own lives that have been impoverished by the waste, and using them in far-spreading blessing and power!

While we have been undervaluing these fractions of eternity, what has our gracious God been doing in them? How strangely touching are the words, "*What is man, that Thou shouldest set Thine heart upon him, and that Thou shouldest visit him every morning, and <u>try him every moment</u>?*" Terribly solemn and awful would be the thought that He has been trying us every moment, were it not for the yearning gentleness and love of the Father revealed in that wonderful expression of wonder, "*What is man, that Thou shouldest set Thine heart upon him?*" Think of that ceaseless setting of His heart upon us, careless and forgetful children as we have been! And then think of those other words, none the less literally true because given. under a figure: *"I, the Lord, do keep it; I will water it every moment."*

We see something of God's infinite greatness and wisdom when we try to fix our dazzled gaze on infinite space. But when we turn to the marvels of the microscope, we gain a clearer view and more definite grasp of these attributes by gazing on the perfection of His infinitesimal handiworks. Just so, while we cannot realize the infinite love which fills eternity, and the infinite vistas of the great future are *"dark with excess of light"* even to the strongest telescopes of faith, we see that love magnified in the microscope of the moments, brought very close to us, and revealing its unspeakable perfection of detail to our wondering sight.

But we do not see this as long as the moments are kept in our own hands. We are like little children closing our fingers over diamonds. How can they receive and reflect the rays of light, analyzing them into all the splendour of their prismatic beauty, while they are kept shut up tight in the dirty little hands? Give them up; let our Father hold them for us, and throw His own great light upon them, and then we shall see them full of fair colours of His manifold loving-kindnesses; and let Him always keep them for us, and then we shall always see His light and His love reflected in them.

And then, surely, they shall be filled with praise. Not that we are to be always singing hymns, and using the expressions of other people's praise, any more than the saints in glory are always literally singing a new song. But praise will be the tone, the colour, the atmosphere in which they flow; none of them away from it or out of it.

Is it a little too much for them all to *"flow in ceaseless praise"*? Well, where will you stop? What proportion of your moments do you think enough for Jesus? How many for the spirit of praise, and how many for the spirit of heaviness? Bl! explicit about it, and come to an understanding. If He is not to have all, then *how much*? Calculate, balance, and apportion. You will not be able to do this in heaven—you know it will be all praise there; but you are free to halve your service of praise here, or to make the proportion what you will.

Yet — He made us for His glory. He chose us that we should be to the praise of His glory. He loves us every moment, waters us every moment, watches us unslumberingly, cares for us unceasingly. Dear friends, I can hardly write this without tears! Shall you or I remember all this love, and hesitate to give all our moments up to Him? Let us entrust Him with them, and ask Him to keep them all — every single one — to Him, and fill them *all* with His praise, and let them *all* be to His praise!

Pondering Points
BY KATIE GARRAWAY

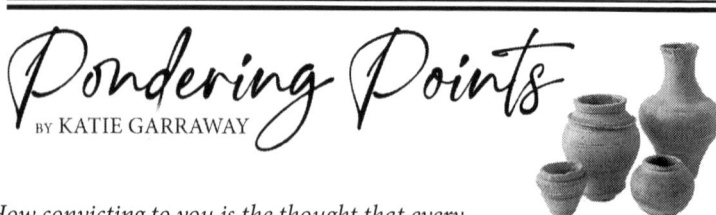

How convicting to you is the thought that every moment matters? Do you seek to make much of the moments that God has given you? There are 86,400 seconds in each day that we live. Are you seeking to spend them wisely and carefully, understanding that time is given to us to be an investment into eternity? Do you look at the little everyday moments in your life and view them as important and potentially life-changing? Do you find yourself squandering your day? Do you waste time throughout your day pointlessly scrolling through social media, strolling through stores aimlessly shopping, or watching television?

God wants us to release into His charge every moment of our time. In what areas is this difficult for you? Are you consciously seeking to live in the moment and live every moment for Him? Do you want God to be involved with each moment? Do you let Him be involved? Or do you selfishly reserve moments throughout your day for yourself and block the Lord out of them? Are you willing to surrender these moments, perhaps used for self or sin, and give them to the One Who gave them to you in the first place? Would you be willing to daily pray, "teach us to number our days, that we may apply our hearts unto wisdom" (Psalm 90:12)*?*

CHAPTER 3
Our Hands Kept For Jesus

*"Keep my hands, that they move
At the impulse of Thy love."*

When the Lord says to us, *"Is thine heart right, as My heart is with thy heart?"* — The next words seem to be, *"If it be, give Me thine hand."* Are you willing to let Him have it and hold it?

What a call to confidence, and love, and free, loyal, happy service is this! and how different will the result of its acceptance be from the old lamentation; *"We labour and have no rest; we have given the hand to the Egyptians and to the Assyrians."* In the service of these *"other lords,"* under whatever shape they have presented themselves, we shall have known something of the meaning of having *"both the hands full with travail and vexation of spirit."* How many a thing have we *"taken in hand,"* as we say, which we expected to find an agreeable task, an interest in life, a something towards filling up that unconfessed aching void which is often most real when least acknowledged; and after a while we have found it change under our hands into irksome travail, involving perpetual vexation of spirit!

The thing may have been of the earth and for the world, and then no wonder it failed to satisfy even the instinct of work, which comes natural to many of us. Or it may have been right enough in itself, something for the good of others so far as we understood their good, and unselfish in all but unraveled motive, and yet we found it full of tangled vexations, because the hands that held it were not simply consecrated to God. Well, if so, let us bring these soiled and tangle-making hands to the Lord, *"Let us lift up our heart with our hands"* to Him, asking Him to clear and cleanse them.

If He says, *"What is that in thine hand?"* — let us examine honestly whether it is something which He can use for His glory or not. If not, do not let us hesitate an instant about dropping it. It may be something we do not like to part with; but the Lord is able to give thee much more than this, and the first glimpse of the excellency of the knowledge of Christ Jesus your Lord will enable us to count those things loss which were gain to us.

But if it is something which He can use, He will make us do ever so much more with it than before. Moses little thought what the Lord was going to make him do with that *"rod in his hand"*! The first thing he had to do with it was to *"cast it on the ground,"* and see it pass through a startling change. After this he was commanded to take it up again, hard and terrifying as it was to do so. But when it became again a rod in his hand, it was no longer what it was before, the simple rod of a wandering desert shepherd. Henceforth it was *"the rod of God in his hand"* (Exodus 4:20), wherewith he should do signs, and by which God Himself would do *"marvellous things"* (Psalm 78:12).

If we look at any Old Testament text about consecration, we shall see that the marginal reading of the word is, *"fill the hand"* (e.g. Exodus 28:41; I Chronicles 29:5). Now, if our hands are full of other things, they cannot be filled with the things that are Jesus Christ's; there must be emptying before there can be any true filling. So if we are sorrowfully seeing that our hands have not been kept for Jesus, let us humbly begin at the beginning, and ask Him to empty them thoroughly, that He may fill them completely. For they *must* be emptied. Either we come to our Lord willingly about it, letting Him unclasp their hold, and gladly dropping the glittering weights they have been carrying, or, in very love, He will have to force them open, and wrench from the reluctant grasp the earthly things which are so occupying them that He cannot have His rightful use of them.

There is only one other alternative, a terrible one, — to be let alone till the day comes when not a gentle Master, but the relentless king of terrors shall empty the trembling hands as our feet follow him out of the busy world into the dark valley, for *"it is certain we can carry nothing out."*

Yet the emptying and the filling are not all that has to be considered. Before the hands of the priests could be filled with the emblems of consecration, they had to be laid upon the emblem of atonement (Leviticus 8:14, etc.). That came first *"Aaron and his sons laid their hands upon the head of the bullock for the sin-offering."* So the transference of guilt to our Substitute (typified by that act) must precede the dedication of ourselves to God. Let us lay our hands humbly upon Christ — *"While like a penitent we stand, and there confess our sin."*

The blood of that Holy Substitute was shed to make reconciliation upon the altar. Without that reconciliation we cannot offer and present ourselves to God; but this being made, Christ Himself presents us. And you, that were sometime alienated, and enemies in your mind by wicked works, yet now hath He reconciled in the body of His flesh through death, to present you holy, unblameable, and unreprovable in His sight.

Then Moses *"brought the ram for the burnt-offering; and Aaron and his sons laid their hands upon the head of the ram, and Moses burnt the whole ram upon the altar; it was a burnt-offering for a sweet savour, and an offering made by fire unto the Lord."* Thus Christ's offering was indeed a whole one, body, soul, and spirit, each and all suffering even unto death. These atoning sufferings, accepted by God for us, are, by our own free act, accepted by us as the ground of our acceptance.

Then, reconciled and accepted, we are ready for consecration; for then *"he brought the other ram; the ram of consecration; and Aaron and his sons laid their hands upon the head of the ram."* Here we see Christ, *"who is consecrated for evermore."* We enter by faith into union with Him who said, *"For their sakes I sanctify Myself, that they also might be sanctified through the truth."*

After all this, their hands were filled with *"consecrations for a sweet savour,"* so, after laying the hand of our faith upon Christ, suffering and dying for us, we are to lay that very same hand of faith, and in the very same way, upon Him as consecrated for us, to be the source and life and power of our consecration. And then our hands shall be filled with consecrations, filled with Christ, and filled with all that is a sweet savour to God in Him.

And who then is willing to fill his hand this day unto the Lord? Do you want an added motive? Listen again: *"Fill your hands to-*

day to the Lord, that He may bestow upon you a blessing this day." Not a long time hence, not even to-morrow, but *"this day".* Do you not want a blessing? Is not your answer to your Father's *"What wilt thou?"* the same as Achsah's, *"Give me a blessing!"* Here is His promise of just what you so want; will you not gladly fulfil His condition? A blessing shall immediately follow. He does not specify what it shall be; Hs waits to reveal it You will find it such a blessing as you had not supposed could be for you — a blessing that shall verily make you rich, with no sorrow added — a blessing *this day*.

All that has been said about consecration applies to our literal members. Stay a minute, and look at your hand, the hand that holds this little book as you read it See how wonderfully it is made; how perfectly fitted for what it has to do; how ingeniously connected with the brain, so as to yield that instantaneous and instinctive obedience without which its beautiful mechanism would be very little good to us! *Your* hand, do you say? Whether it is soft and fair with an easy life, or rough and strong with a working one, or white and weak with illness, it is the Lord Jesus Christ's. It is not your own at all; it belongs to Him. He made it, for without Him was not anything made that was made, not even your hand. And He has the added right of purchase — He has bought it that it might be one of His own instruments. We know this very well, but have we realized it? Have we really let Him have the use of these hands of ours? and have we ever simply and sincerely asked Him to keep them for His own use?

Does this mean that we are always to be doing some definitely "religious" work, as it is called? No, but that *all that we do* is to be always definitely done *for Him*. There is a great difference. If the hands are indeed moving *"at the impulse of His love,"* the simplest little duties and acts are transfigured into Holy service to the Lord.

> *A servant with this clause*
> *Makes drudgery divine;*
> *Who sweeps a room as for Thy laws,*
> *Makes that and the action fine.*

A Christian schoolgirl loves Jesus; she wants to please Him all day long, and so she practices her scales carefully and conscientiously. It is at the impulse of His love that her fingers move so steadily through the otherwise tiresome exercises. Someday her Master will find a use for her music; but meanwhile it may be just as really done unto Him as if it were Mr. Sankey at his organ, swaying the hearts of thousands. The hand of a Christian lad traces his Latin verses, or his figures, or his copying. He is doing his best, because a banner has been given him that it may be displayed, not so much by talk as by continuance in well-doing. And so, for Jesus' sake, his hand moves accurately and perseveringly.

A busy wife, or daughter, or servant has a number of little manual duties to perform. If these are done slowly and leisurely, they may be got through, but there will not be time left for some little service to the poor, or some little kindness to a suffering or troubled neighbour, or for a little quiet time alone with God and His word. And so the hands move quickly, impelled by the loving desire for service or communion, kept in busy motion for Jesus' sake. Or it may be that the special aim is to give no occasion of reproach to some who are watching, but so to adorn the doctrine that those may be won by the life who will not be won by the word. Then the hands will have their share to do; they will move carefully, neatly, perhaps even elegantly, making everything around as nice as possible, letting their intelligent touch be seen in the details of the home, and even of the dress, doing or arranging all the little things decently and in order for Jesus' sake. And so on with every duty in every position.

It may seem an odd idea, but a simple glance at one's hand, with the recollection, *"This hand is not mine; it has been given to Jesus, and it must be kept for Jesus,"* may sometimes turn the scale in a doubtful matter and be a safeguard from certain temptations. With that thought fresh in your mind as you look at your hand, can you let it take up things which, to say the very least, are not *"for Jesus"*? things which evidently cannot be used, as they most certainly are not used, either for Him or by Him?

Gambling cards, for instance, used for any pastime yet by association is a part of the evil it represents! Or can you deliberately hold in your hands books of a kind which you know perfectly well, by sadly repeated experience, lead you farther from instead of nearer to Him? books which must and do fill your mind with those *"other things"* which, entering in, choke the word? Books which you would not care to read at all, if your heart were burning within you at the coming of His feet to bless you? Next time any temptation of this sort approaches, just *look at your hand!*

It was of a literal hand that our Lord Jesus spoke when He said, "Behold, the hand of him that betrayeth Me is with Me on the table;" and, "He that dippeth his hand with Me in the dish, the same shall betray Me." A hand so near to Jesus, with Him on the table, touching His own hand in the dish at that hour of sweetest, and closest, and most solemn intercourse, and yet betraying Him! That same hand taking the thirty pieces of silver! What a tremendous lesson of the need of keeping for our hands! Oh that every hand that is with Him at His sacramental table, and that takes the memorial bread, may be kept from any faithless and loveless motion! And again, it was by literal *wicked hands* that our Lord Jesus was crucified and slain. Does not the thought that human hands have been so treacherous and cruel to our beloved Lord make us wish the more fervently that out hands may be totally faithful and devoted to Him?

Danger and temptation to let the hands move at other impulses is every bit as great to those who have nothing else to do but to render direct service, and who think they are doing nothing else. Take one practical instance — our letter-writing. Have we not been tempted (and fallen before the temptation), according to our various dispositions, to let the hand that holds the pen move at the impulse to write an unkind thought of another; or to say a clever and sarcastic thing, or a slightly coloured and exaggerated thing, which will make our point more telling; or to let out a grumble or a suspicion; or to let the pen run away with us into flippant and trifling words, unworthy of our high and Holy calling? Have we not drifted away from the golden reminder, *"Should he reason with unprofitable talk, and with speeches wherewith he can do no good?"* Why has this been, perhaps again and again? Is it not for want of putting our hands into our dear Master's hand, and asking and trusting Him to keep them? He could have kept; He *would* have kept!

Whatever our work or our special temptations may be, the principle remains the same, only let us apply it for ourselves.

Perhaps one hardly needs to say that the kept hands will be very gentle hands. Quick, angry motions of the heart will sometimes force themselves into expression by the hand, though the tongue may be restrained. The very way in which we close a door or lay down a book may be a victory or a defeat, a witness to Christ's keeping or a witness that we are not truly being kept How can we expect that God will use this member as an instrument of righteousness unto Him, if we yield it thus as an instrument of unrighteousness unto sin? Therefore let us see to it, that it is at once yielded to Him whose right it is; and let our sorrow that it should have been even for an instant desecrated to Satan's use, lead us to entrust it henceforth to our Lord to be kept by the power of God through faith *"for the Master's use."*

For when the gentleness of Christ dwells in us, He can use the merest touch of a finger. Have we not heard of one gentle touch on a wayward shoulder being the turning-point of a life? I have known a case in which the Master made use of Jess than that — only the quiver of a little finger being made the means of touching a wayward heart.

What must the touch of the Master's own hand have been! One imagines it very gentle, though so full of power. Can He not communicate both the power and the gentleness? When He touched the hand of Peter's wife's mother, she arose and ministered unto them. Do you not think the hand which Jesus had just touched must have ministered very excellently? As we ask Him to touch our lips with living fire, so that they may speak effectively for Him, may we not ask Him to touch our hands, that they may minister effectively, and excel in all that they find to do for Him? Then our hands shall be made strong by the hands of the Mighty God of Jacob.

It is very pleasant to feel that if our hands are indeed our Lord's, we may ask Him to guide them, and strengthen them, and teach them. I do not mean figuratively, but quite literally. In everything they do for Him (and that should be *everything we ever undertake*) we want to do it well-better and better. *"Seek that ye may excel."* We are too apt to think that He has given us certain natural gifts, but has nothing practically to do with the improvement of them, and leaves us to ourselves for that. Why not ask Him to make these hands of ours more handy for His service, more skillful in what is indicated as the *"next thing"* they are to do? The *kept* hands need not be clumsy hands. If the Lord taught David's hands to war and his fingers to fight, will He not teach our hands, and fingers too, to do what He would have them do?

The Spirit of God must have taught Bezaleel's hands as well as his head, for he was filled with it not only that he might devise cunning works, but also in cutting of stones and carving of timber. And when all the women that were wise-hearted did spin with their hands, the hands must have been made skillful as well as the hearts made wise to prepare the beautiful garments and curtains.

There is a very remarkable instance of the hand of the Lord, which I suppose signifies in that case the power of His Spirit, being upon the hand of a man. In I Chronicles 28:19, we read: *"All this, said David, the Lord made me understand in writing by His hand upon me, even all the works of this pattern."* This cannot well mean that the Lord gave David a miraculously written scroll, because, a few verses before it says that he had it all by the Spirit So what else can it mean but that as David wrote, the hand of the Lord was upon his hand, impelling him to trace, letter by letter, the right words of description for all the details of the temple that Solomon should build, with its courts and chambers, its treasuries and vessels? Have we not sometimes sat down to write, feeling perplexed and ignorant, and wishing someone were there to tell us what to say? At such a moment, whether it were a mere note for post, or a sheet for press, it is a great comfort to recollect this mighty laying of a Divine hand upon a human one, and ask for the same help from the same Lord. It is sure to be given!

And now, dear friend, what about your own hands? Are they consecrated to the Lord who loves you? And if they are, are you trusting Him to keep them, and enjoying all that is involved in that keeping? Do let this be settled with your Master before you go on to the next chapter.

After all, this question will hinge on another, *Do you love Him?* If you really do, there can surely be neither hesitation about yielding them to Him, nor about entrusting them to Him to be kept. *Does He love you?* That is the truer way of putting it; for it is not our love to Christ, but the love of Christ to us which constraineth us. And this is the impulse of the motion and the mode of the keeping. The steam engine does not move when the fire is not kindled, nor when it is gone out; no matter how complete the machinery and abundant the fuel, cold coals will neither set it going nor keep it working. Let us ask Him so to shed abroad His love in our hearts by the Holy Ghost which is given unto us, that it may be the perpetual and only impulse of every action of our daily life.

Pondering Points
BY KATIE GARRAWAY

Do you seek to be clean in all that you do with your hands? James 4:8 plainly says, "Draw nigh to God, and he will draw nigh to you. **Cleanse your hands, ye sinners;** *and purify your hearts, ye double minded." What are you doing with your hands? Many impure and inappropriate things can be done with our hands. We must never forget that the actions of our hands are the outward extension of the intentions of our hearts. In a moment of consecration, yield your hands to Jesus. "Please TAKE them and KEEP them, Lord, for Thy glory!"*

What is in your hand? There can never be a filling of the things which are Christ's if our hands are already full of the things of the world or our own selfish pleasure. Ask God to help you do everything for Him. Remember, what we might consider the simple mundane tasks of our day-to-day lives, if moving at the impulse of His love, can actually be acts of service to Him!

Do you strive for excellence in every undertaking with your hands? Ecclesiastes 9:10 exhorts us, "Whatsoever thy hand findeth to do, do it with thy might." Or do you find yourself settling for mediocrity? Let us daily ask the Lord to guide, strengthen and teach our hands that we may do our task better and better for His glory. Maybe it's playing a musical instrument, sewing a garment, teaching your children, working at home or at your job or decorating your house or Sunday School classroom — may our hands be dedicated to Christ and always striving to do their best for Him.

CHAPTER 4
Our Feet Kept For Jesus

*"Keep my feet, that they may be
Swift and beautiful for Thee."*

The figurative keeping of the feet of His saints, with the promise that when they run they shall not stumble, is a most beautiful and helpful subject. But it is quite distinct from the literal keeping for Jesus of our literal feet.

There is a certain homeliness about the idea which helps to make it very real. These very feet of ours are purchased for Christ's service by the precious drops which fell from His own term and pierced feet upon the cross. They are to be His errand-runners. How can we let the world, the flesh, and the devil have the use of what has been purchased with such payment?

Shall **THE WORLD** have the use of them? Shall they carry us where the world is paramount, and the Master cannot be even named, because the mention of His Name would be so obviously out of place? I know the apparent difficulties of a subject which will at once occur in connection with this, but they all vanish when our bright banner is loyally unfurled, with its motto, *"All for Jesus!"* Do you honestly want your very feet to be kept for Jesus? Let these simple words, *"Kept for Jesus"*, ring out next time you wish to dance or perform any other worldly amusement with your feet, and I know what the result will be!

Shall **THE FLESH** have the use of them? Shall they carry us hither and thither merely because we like to go, merely because it pleases ourselves to take this walk or pay this visit? And after all, what a failure it is! If people only *would* believe it, self-pleasing is always a failure in the end. Our good Master gives us a reality and fullness of *pleasure* in pleasing Him which we never get out of pleasing ourselves.

Shall **THE DEVIL** have the use of them? Oh no, of course not! We start back at this, as a highly unnecessary question. Yet if Jesus has not, Satan has. For as all are serving either the Prince of Life or the prince of this world, and as no man can serve two masters, it follows that if we are not serving the one, we are serving the other. And Satan is only too glad to disguise this service under the less startling form of the world, or the still less startling one of self. All that is not *"kept for Jesus,"* is left for self or the world, and therefore for Satan.

There is no fear but that our Lord will have many uses for what is kept by Him for Himself. *"How beautiful are the feet of them that bring glad tidings of good things!"* That is the best use of all; and I expect the angels think those feet beautiful, even if they are cased in muddy boots or goloshes.

Once the question was asked, *"Wherefore wilt thou run, my son, seeing that thou hast no tidings ready?"* So, if we want to have these beautiful feet, we must have the tidings ready which they are to bear. Let us ask Him to keep our hearts so freshly full of His good news of salvation, that our mouths may speak out of their abundance. *"If the clouds be full of rain, they empty themselves upon the earth."* The *"two olive branches empty the golden oil out of themselves."* May we be so filled with the Spirit that we may thus have much to pour out for others!

Besides the great privilege of carrying water from the wells of salvation, there are plenty of cups of cold water to be carried in all directions; not to the poor only — ministries of love are often as much needed by a rich friend. But the feet must be kept for these; they will be too tired for them if they are tired out for self-pleasing. In such services, we are treading in the blessed steps of His most Holy life, who went about doing good.

Then there is literal errand-going — just to fetch something that is needed for the household, or something that a tired relative wants, whether asked or unasked. Such things should come first instead of last, because these are clearly indicated as our Lord's will for us to do, by the position in which He has placed us; while what seems more direct service, maybe after all not so directly apportioned by Him. *"I have to go and buy some soap,"* said one with a little sigh. The sigh was waste of breath, for her feet were going to do her Lord's will for that next half-hour much more truly than if they had carried her to her well-worked district, and left the soap to take its chance.

May it not be a comfort to those of us who feel we have not the mental or spiritual power that others have, to notice that the living sacrifice mentioned in Romans 12:1 is our bodies. Of course, that includes the mental power, but does it not also include the loving, sympathizing glance, the kind, encouraging word, *the ready errand for another*, the work of our hands, opportunities for all of which come oftener in the day than for the mental power we are often tempted to envy? May we be enabled to offer willingly that which we have. For if there be first a willing mind, it is accepted according to that a man hath, and not according to that he hath not.

If our feet are to be kept at His disposal, our eyes must be ever toward the Lord for guidance. We must look to Him for our orders where to go. Then He will be sure to give them. *"The steps of a good man are ordered by the Lord."* Very often we find that they have been so very literally ordered for us that we are quite astonished — just as if He had not promised!

Do not smile at a *very* homely thought! If our feet are not our own, ought we not to take care of them for Him whose they are? Is it quite right to be reckless about getting "wet feet", which might be guarded against either by forethought or afterthought, when there is, at least, a risk of hindering our service thereby? Does it please the Master when even in our zeal for His work we annoy anxious friends by carelessness in little things of this kind?

May every step of our feet be more and more like those of our beloved Master. Let us continually consider Him in this, and go where He would have gone, on the errands which He would have done, *"following hard"* after Him. And let us look on to the time when our feet shall stand in the gates of the heavenly Jerusalem, when Holy feet shall tread the streets of the Holy City; no longer pacing any lonely path, for He hath said, *"They shall walk with Me in white."*

> *And He hath said, "How beautiful the feet!"*
> *The "feet" so weary, travel-stained, and worn—*

Devotional Inspired by "Take My Life & Let It Be"

---

*The "feet" that humbly, patiently have borne
The toilsome way, the pressure, and the heat.*

*The "feet," not hasting on with winged might,
Nor strong to trample down the opposing foe;
So lowly, and so human, they must go
By painful steps to scale the mountain height.*

*Not unto all the tuneful lips are given,
The ready tongue, the words so strong and sweet;
Yet all may turn, with humble, willing "feet,"
And bear to darkened souls the light from heaven.*

*And fall they while the goal far distant lies,
With scarce a word yet spoken for their Lord
His sweet approval He doth yet accord;
Their "feet" are beauteous in the Master's eyes.*

*With weary human "feet" He, day by day,
Once trod this earth to work His acts of love;
And every step is chronicled above
His servants take to follow in His way.*

Pondering Points
BY KATIE GARRAWAY

Are we swift to run and do things for ourselves and slow to run for our Saviour? Do we use our feet to further the wicked work of gossip or the wonderful work of the Gospel? Are our feet too tired out from pleasing self to run to the aid of someone else in need? Or too busy running to and fro with trivial self-absorbed tasks that we completely miss the opportunity to serve someone else?

Psalm 37:23 says, "The steps of a good man are ordered by the Lord." Are we looking to Him so He can order our steps day by day? Are we willing to allow the Lord to rearrange our day and "inconvenience" our schedule to direct our feet in the "paths of righteousness for His name's sake"? Do we recognize that we can very easily take the wrong steps? Are we actively praying each day for the Lord to guide our feet? Or is our focus so distracted that His leading, direction, and orders go unheeded and ignored?

CHAPTER 5
Our Voices Kept For Jesus

*"Keep my voice, and let me sing
Always, only, for my King."*

I have wondered a little at being told by an experienced worker, that in many cases the voice seems the last and hardest thing to yield entirely to the King; and that many who think and say they have consecrated all to the Lord and His service, revolt when it comes to be a question of whether they shall sing *"always, only,"* for their King. They do not mind singing a few general sacred songs, but they do not see their way to really singing always and only unto and for Him. They want to bargain and balance a little. They question and argue about what proportion they may keep for self-pleasing and company-pleasing, and how much they must give up; and who will and who won't like it; and what they really *"must sing,"* and what they really must sing at certain times and places; and what *"won't do,"* and what they *"can't very well help,"* and so on. And so when the question, *"How much owest thou unto my Lord?"* is applied to this particularly pleasant gift, it is not met with the loyal, free-hearted, happy response, "*All! yes, all for Jesus!*"

I know there are special temptations around this matter:

- **Vain and selfish ones** — whispering how much better a certain song suits your voice, and how much more likely to be admired.
- **Faithless ones** — suggesting doubts whether you can make the Holy song sound forth and it truly be a spiritual blessing to the hearers of it.
- **Specious ones** — asking whether you ought not to please your neighbours, and hushing up the rest of the precept, "*Let every one of you please his neighbour for his good to edification*" (Romans 15:2).
- **Cowardly ones** — telling you that it is just a little too much to expect of you, and that you are not called upon to wave your banner in people's very faces, and provoke surprise and remark, as this might do. And so the banner is kept furled, the witness for Jesus is not borne, and you sing for others and not for your God and King.

The words had passed your lips — "*Take my voice!*" — and yet you will not let Him have it; you will not let Him have that which costs you something, just *because* it costs you something! And yet He lent you that pleasant voice that you might use it for Him. And yet He, in the sureness of His perpetual presence, was beside you all the while, and heard every note as you sang the songs which were, as your inmost heart knew, *not* for Him.

Where is your faith? Where is the consecration you have talked about? The voice has not been kept for Him, because it has not been truly and unreservedly given to Him. Will you not now say, *"Take my voice, for I had not given it to Thee; keep my voice, for I cannot keep it for Thee"*?

And He will keep it! You cannot tell, till you have tried, how surely all the temptations flee when it is no longer your battle but the Lord's; nor how completely and *curiously* all the difficulties vanish, when you simply and trustfully go forward in the path of full consecration in this matter. You will find that the keeping is most wonderfully real. Do not expect to lay down rules and provide for every sort of contingency. If you could, you would miss the sweetness of the continual guidance in the "kept" course. Have only one rule about it — just to look up to your Master about every single song you are asked or feel inclined to sing. If you are *"willing and obedient,"* you will always meet His guiding eye. He will always keep the voice that is wholly at His disposal. Soon you will have such experience of His immediate guidance that you will be utterly satisfied with it, and only sorrowfully wonder you did not sooner thus simply lean on it

I have just received a letter from one who has laid her special gift at the feet of the Giver, yielding her voice to Him with hearty desire that it might be kept for His use. She wrote: *"I had two lessons on singing while in Germany from our Master. One was very sweet A young girl wrote to me, that when she had heard me sing, 'O come, everyone that thirsteth,' she went away and prayed that she might come, and she did come, too. Is not He good? The other was: I had been tempted to join the <u>Gesang Verein</u> in N—. I prayed to be shown whether I was right in so doing or not I did* not see my way clear, so I went. The singing was all secular. The very first night I went and caught a bad cold on my chest, which prevented me from singing again at all till Christmas. Those were better than any lessons from a singing master!"

Does not this illustrate both the keeping *from* and the keeping *for*? In the latter case I believe she honestly wished to know her Lord's will — whether the training and practice were needed for His better service with her music — and that, therefore, she might take them for His sake. Or whether the accompaniments, influence, and musical form would be such as to *hinder* the close communion with Him Who she had found so precious; and that, therefore, she was to trust Him to give her *"much more than this."* And so, at once, He showed her unmistakably what He would have her not do and gave her the sweet consciousness that He Himself was teaching her and taking her at her word. I know what her passionate love for music is, and how very real and great the compensation from Him must have been which could thus make her right down glad about what would otherwise have been an immense disappointment.

And then, as to the former of these two lessons, the song she names was one substituted when, she said, *"Take my voice,"* for some which were far more effective for her voice. But having freely chosen to sing what might glorify the Master rather than the singer, see how, almost immediately, He gave her a reward infinitely outweighing all the drawing-room compliments or concert-room applause! That one consecrated song found echoes in heaven, bringing, by its blessed result, joy to the angels and glory to God. And the memory of that song is immortal; it will live through ages to come, never lost, never dying away, when the vocal triumphs of the world's greatest singers are past and forgotten forever. Now you who have been taking a half-and-half course, do you get such rewards as this? You may well envy them! But why not take the same decided course, and share the same blessed keeping and its fulness of hidden reward?

If you only knew, dear hesitating friends, what strength and gladness the Master gives when we loyally *"sing forth the honour of His Name,"* you would not forego it! Oh, if you only knew the difficulties it saves! For when you sing *"always and only for your King,"* you will not get much entangled by the King's enemies.

Singing an out-and-out sacred song often clears one's path at a stroke as to many other things. If you only knew the rewards He gives — very often then and there; the recognition that you are one of the King's friends by some lonely and timid one; the openings which you quite naturally gain of speaking a word for Jesus to hearts which, without the song, would never have given you the chance of the word! If you only knew the joy of believing that His sure promise — *"My Word shall not return unto Me void"* — will be fulfilled as you *sing* that word for Him! If you only tasted the solemn happiness of knowing that you have indeed a royal audience, that the King Himself is listening as you sing! If you only knew — and why should you not know? Shall not the time past of your life suffice you for the miserable, double-hearted, calculating service? Let Him have the *whole* use of your voice at any cost and see if He does not put many a totally unexpected new song into your mouth!

I am not writing all this to great and finished singers, but to everybody who can sing at all. Those who think they have only a very small talent, are often most tempted not to trade with it for their Lord. Whether you have much or little natural voice, there is reason for its cultivation and room for its use. Place it at your Lord's disposal, and He will show you how to make the most of it for Him; for not seldom His multiplying power is brought to bear on a consecrated voice. A puzzled singing master, very famous in his profession, said to one who tried to sing for Jesus; *"Well, you have not much voice; but, mark my words, you will always beat anybody with four times your voice!"* He was right, though he did not in the least know why.

A great many so-called "sacred songs" are so plaintive and pathetic that they help to give a gloomy idea of religion. Don't sing these — come out boldly, and sing definitely and unmistakeably for your King, and of your King, and to your King. You will soon find, and even outsiders will have to own, that it is a good thing thus to show forth His loving-kindness and His faithfulness (see Psalm 92:1-3).

Here I am usually met by the query, *"But what would you advise me to sing?"* I can only say that I never got any practical help from asking anyone but the Master Himself, and so I would advise you to do the same! He knows exactly what will best suit your voice and enable you to sing best for Him; for He made it and gave it just the pitch and tone He pleased, so, of course, He is the best counsellor about it. Refer your question in simplest faith to Him, and I am perfectly sure you will find it answered. He will direct you, and in some way or other the Lord will provide the right songs for you to sing. That is the very best advice I can possibly give you on the subject, and you will prove it to be so if you will act upon it.

Only one thing I would add: **I believe there is nothing like singing His own words.** The preacher claims the promise, *"My Word shall not return unto Me void,"* and why should not the singer equally claim it? Why should we use His own inspired words with faith in their power, when speaking or writing, and content ourselves with human words put into rhyme (and sometimes very feeble rhyme) for our singing?

What a vista of happy work opens out here! What is there to prevent our using this mightiest of all agencies committed to human agents, the Word, which is quick and powerful, and sharper than any two-edged sword, whenever we are asked to sing? By this means, even a young girl may be privileged to make that Word sound in the ears of many who would not listen to it otherwise. By this, the incorruptible seed may be sown in otherwise unreachable ground.

It is a remarkable fact that it is actually the easiest way thus to take the very highest ground You will find that singing Bible words does not excite the prejudice or contempt that any other words, sufficiently decided to be worth singing, are almost sure to do. For very decency's sake, a Bible song will be listened to respectfully; and for very shame's sake, no adverse whisper will be ventured against the words in ordinary English homes. The singer is placed on a vantage-ground, certain that at least the words of the song will be outwardly respected, and the possible ground of unfriendly criticism thus narrowed to begin with.

But there is much more than this. One feels the power of His words for oneself as one sings. One loves them and rejoices in them, and what can be greater help to any singer than that? And one knows they are true, and that they cannot really return void, and what can give greater confidence than that? God *may* bless the singing of any words, but He *must* bless the singing of His own Word, if that promise means what it says!

The only real difficulty in the matter is that Scripture songs, as a rule, require a little more practice than others. Then practice them a little more! You think nothing of the trouble of learning, for instance, a sonata, which takes you many a good hour's practice before you can render it perfectly and expressively. But you shrink from a song, the accompaniment of which you cannot read off without any trouble at all. And you never think of such a thing as taking one-tenth the pains to learn that accompaniment that you took to learn that sonata! Very likely, too, you take the additional pains to learn the sonata off by heart, so that you may play it more effectively. But you do not take pains to learn your accompaniment by heart, so that you may throw all your power into the expression of the words, undistracted by reading the notes and turning over the leaves. It is far more useful to have half a dozen Scripture songs thoroughly learnt and made your own, than to have in your portfolios several dozen easy settings of sacred poetry which you get through with your eyes fixed on the notes. And everyone thus thoroughly mastered makes it easier to master others.

You will say that all this refers only to drawing-room singing. So it does, primarily, but then it is the drawing-room singing which has been so little for Jesus and so much for self and society; and so much less has been said about it, and so much less done. There would not be half the complaints of the difficulty of witnessing for Christ in even professedly Christian homes and circles, if every converted singer were also a consecrated one. For nothing raises or lowers the tone of a whole evening so much as the character of the music. There are few things which show more clearly that, as a rule, a very definite step in advance is needed beyond being a. believer or even a worker for Christ Over how many grand or cottage pianos could the Irish Society's motto, *"For Jesus' sake only,"* be hung, without being either a frequent reproach, or altogether inappropriate?

But what is learnt will, naturally, be sung. And oh! How many Christian parents give their daughters the advantage of singing lessons without troubling themselves in the least about what songs are learnt, provided they are not exceptionally foolish! Still more pressingly I would say, how many Christian principals, to whom young lives are entrusted at the most important time of all for training, do not give themselves the least concern about this matter!

As I write, I turn aside to refer to a list of songs learnt last term by a fresh young voice which would willingly be trained for higher work. There is just one sacred song in the whole long list, and even that hardly such a one as the writer of the letter above quoted would care to sing in her fervent-spirited service of Christ. All the rest are harmless and pleasing, but only suggestive of the things of earth, the things of the world that is passing away; not one that might lead upward and onward, not one that might touch a careless heart to seek first the kingdom of God, not one that might show forth the glory and praise of our King, not one that tells out His grace and love, not one that carries His comfort to His weary ones or His joy to His loving ones. She is left to find and learn such songs as best she may; those which she will sing with all the ease and force gained by good teaching of them are no help at all, but rather hindrance in anything like wish or attempt to *"sing for Jesus."*

There is not the excuse that the songs of God's kingdom, songs which waft His own words to the souls around, would not have answered the teacher's purpose as well. God has taken care of that. He has not left Himself without witness in this direction. He has given the most perfect melodies and the richest harmonies to be linked with His own words, and no singer can be trained beyond His wonderful provision in this way. I pray that even these poor words of mine may reach the consciences of some of those who have this responsibility and lead them to be no longer unfaithful in this important matter, no longer giving this strangely divided service — training, as they profess to desire, the souls for God, and yet allowing the voices to be trained only for the world.

But we must not run away with the idea that singing sacred songs and singing for Jesus are convertible terms. I know by sorrowful personal experience that it is very possible to sing a sacred song and *not* sing it for Jesus. It is easier to have one's portfolio all right than one's heart, and the repertory is more easily arranged than the motives. When we have taken our side, and the difficulties of indecision are consequently swept away, we have a new set of more subtle temptations to encounter. And although the Master will keep, the servant must watch and pray; and it is through the watching and the praying that the keeping will be effectual. We have, however, rather less excuse here than even elsewhere. For we never have to sing so very suddenly that we need be taken unawares.

We have to think carefully in the Spirit what to sing, and perhaps find the music, and the prelude has to be played, and all this gives quite enough time for us to recollect whose we are and Whom we serve, and to arouse to the watch. Quite enough, too, for trustful prayer that our singing may be kept free from that wretched self-seeking or even self-consciousness, and kept entirely for Jesus. Our best and happiest singing will flow when there is a sweet, silent undercurrent of prayerful or praiseful communion with our Master all through the song. As for nervousness, I am quite sure this is the best antidote to that

On the other hand, it is quite possible to sing for Jesus without singing a sacred song. Do not take an ell for the inch this seems to give, and run off with the idea that it does not matter after all what you sing, so that you sing in a good frame of mind! **No such thing!** And the admission needs very careful guarding and must not be wrested into an excuse for looking back to the world's songs. But cases may and do arise in which it may be right to gratify a weary father, or win a wayward brother, by trying to please them with music to which they will listen when they would not listen to the songs you would rather sing. There are cases in which this may be done most truly for the Lord's sake, and clearly under His guidance.

Sometimes cases arise in which we can only say, *"Neither know we what to do, but our eyes are upon Thee."* And when we honestly say that, depend upon it we shall find the promise true, *"I will guide thee with Mine eye."* For God is faithful, who will not suffer you to be tempted above that ye are able, but will, with the temptation, also make a way to escape, that ye may be able to bear it. (See I Corinthians 10:13.)

I do not know why it should be so, but it certainly is a much rarer thing to find a young gentleman singing for Jesus than a young lady, — a *very* rare thing to find one with a cultivated voice consecrating it to the Master's use. I have met some who were not ashamed to speak for Him, to whom it never seemed even to occur to sing for Him. They would go and teach a Bible class one day, and the next they would be practicing or performing just the same songs as those who care nothing for

Christ and His blood-bought salvation. They had left some things behind, but they had not left any of their old songs behind. They do not seem to think that being made new creatures in Christ Jesus had anything to do with this department of their lives. Nobody could gather whether they were on the Lord's side or not, as they stood and sang their neutral songs. The banner that was displayed in the class-room was furled in the drawing-room.

Now, my friends, you who have or may have far greater opportunities of displaying that banner than we womenkind, why should you be less brave and loyal than your sisters? We are weak and you are strong naturally but recollect that want of decision always involves want of power, and compromising Christians are always weak Christians. You will never be mighty to the pulling down of strongholds while you have one foot in the enemy's camp, or on the supposed neutral ground, if such can exist (which I doubt), between the camps. You will never be a terror to the devil till you have enlisted every gift and faculty on the Lord's side. Here is a thing in which you may practically carry out the splendid motto, *"All for Jesus."* You cannot be all for Him as long as your voice is not for Him. Which shall it be? *All* for Him, or *partly* for Him? Answer that to Him whom you call Master and Lord.

When once this drawing-room question is settled, there is not much need to expatiate about other forms of singing for Jesus. As we have opportunity, we shall be willing to do good with our pleasant gift in any way or place, and it is wonderful what nice opportunities He makes for us. Whether to one little sick child or to a thousand listeners, according to the powers and openings granted, we shall take our happy position among those who minister with singing (1 Chron. 6. 32). And in so far as we really do this unto the Lord, I am quite sure He gives the hundred-fold now in this present time more than all the showy songs or self-gratifying performances we may have left for His sake. As we steadily tread this part of the path of consecration, we shall find the difficulties left behind, and the real pleasantness of the way reached, and it will be a delight to say to oneself, *"I cannot sing the old songs;"* and though you have thought it quite enough to say, *"With my song will I please my friends,"* especially if they happen to be pleased with a mildly sacred song or two, you will strike a higher and happier, a richer and purer note, and say with David, *"With my song will I praise Him."* David said also, *"My lips shall, greatly rejoice when I sing unto Thee, and my soul, which Thou hast redeemed."* And you will find that this comes true.

> *Singing for Jesus, our Saviour and King;*
> *Singing for Jesus, the Lord whom we love!*
> *All adoration we joyously bring,*
> *Longing to praise as they praise Him above.*

> *Singing for Jesus, our Shepherd and Guide;*
> *Singing for gladness of heart that He gives;*
> *Singing for wonder and praise that He died;*
> *Singing for blessing and joy that He lives!*

> *Singing for Jesus, and trying to win*
> *Many to love Him, and join in the song;*
> *Calling the weary and wandering in,*
> *Rolling the chorus of gladness along.*

Pondering Points
BY KATIE GARRAWAY

The voice is an instrument that God created within our bodies for us to use for His glory. The Bible exhorts us in I Corinthians 6:19-20, "What? know ye not that your body is the temple of the Holy Ghost which is in you, which ye have of God, and ye are not your own? For ye are bought with a price: therefore glorify God in your body, and in your spirit, which are God's." There should be no question or hesitation that our voices should be used "all for Jesus" — kept for His use. Certainly, the world should <u>not</u> be confused by hearing two different sounds or songs coming from the voice of the believer. This creates confusion, and God is not the author of confusion (I Corinthians 14:33).

Do you ask yourself these questions: As I am singing for Jesus, how am I using my voice when I sing? Does my singing and the use of my voice appeal to the flesh or the spirit? What does my voice sound like? Does the style I use match the sacredness of the words which I am singing?

Believe it or not, there is a right way and a wrong way to sing. Husky, guttural, breathy, "close", and raspy singing are all methods and styles developed and made popular by the world. Unfortunately, these same methods used by secular artists to make a sensual and breathy sound are being used in churches today. Yet many Christians either do not realize it or deliberately ignore it. (We are not speaking about "grace notes" [an extra note added as an artistic embellishment though not essential to the harmony or melody] or the use of "portamento" [meaning "carriage" or "carrying"; a purposeful slide from one note to the other]. These and other musical "ornaments" can be utilized skillfully and conscientiously without evoking a sensual feeling.)

The <u>sound</u> of the voice itself suggests what a singer truly means. Through it, a secondary message is being conveyed to the listener besides just the words they hear sung. Jesus said in Matthew 12:34, "...out of the abundance of the heart the mouth speaketh." When you sing, what sort of message are you sharing? Ephesians 4:29 declares, "Let no corrupt communication proceed out of your mouth, but that which is good to the use of edifying, that it may minister grace unto the hearers."

Certainly, there are different singing styles; God is not looking for us to be identical as robots — we are all created differently! But, we must determine if the style we are engaging in mimics anything sensual or secular. God's people aren't to imitate the world or copy its "sound." God wants the melody we make to glorify Him and to be pure and certain (Ephesians 5:19). Galatians 5:24 states, "And they that are Christ's have crucified the flesh with the affections and lusts."

When you sing, do you consider if it pleases and glorifies God or appeals to and gratifies the flesh? Ask God to help your voice be free of self-consciousness and anything self-seeking. May we sing with a sweet, silent undercurrent of prayerful, praise-filled communion with Him all throughout the song. This will be a great help to eliminate the flesh (and even nervousness) and keep our focus on the One we are singing for!

I encourage you to consider reading our book "A Biblical Approach to Music" that gives a thorough explanation of this subject. It is a Scriptural, practical, thought-provoking, authentic, well-documented and highly-recommended resource that will greatly help you in your pursuit of Christ-honoring music. You can purchase it from our website: remnantministriesonline.com, or in person at one of our revival meetings.

CHAPTER 6
Our Lips Kept For Jesus

*"Keep my lips, that they may be
Filled with messages from Thee."*

The days are past forever when we said, *"Our lips are our own."* We now know that they are not our own.

And yet how many of my readers often have the miserable consciousness that they have spoken unadvisedly with their lips! How many pray, *"Keep the door of my lips,"* when the very last thing they think of expecting is that they *will* be kept! They deliberately make up their minds that hasty words, or foolish words, or exaggerated words, according to their respective temptations, must and will slip out of that door, and that it can't be helped. The extent of the real meaning of their prayer was merely that not quite so many might slip out. As their faith went no farther, the answer went no farther, and so the door was not kept.

Do let us look the matter straight in the face. Either we have committed our lips to our Lord, or we have not This question must be settled first If not, oh, do not let another hour pass! Take them to Jesus, and ask Him to take them.

But when you *have* committed them to Him, it comes to this — is He able or is He not able to keep that which you have committed to Him? If He is not able, of course you may as well give up at once, for your own experience has abundantly proved that you are not able, so there is no help for you. But if He is able — nay, thank God there is no *if* on this side! — say, rather, as He is able, where was this inevitable necessity of perpetual failure? You have been fancying yourself virtually doomed and fated to it, and therefore you have gone on in it, while all the time His arm was not shortened that it could not save, but you have been limiting the Holy One of Israel. Honestly, now, have you trusted Him to keep your lips this day? Trust necessarily implies expectation that what we have entrusted will be kept If you have not expected Him to keep, you have not trusted. You may have tried, and tried very hard, but you have not trusted, and therefore you have not been kept, and your lips have been the snare of your soul (Proverbs 18:7).

Once I heard a beautiful prayer which I can never forget; it was this: *"Lord, take my lips, and speak through them; take my mind, and think through it; take my heart, and set it on fire."* And this is the way the Master keeps the lips of His servants, by so filling their hearts with His love that the outflow cannot be unloving, by so filling their thoughts that the utterance cannot be un-Christ-like. There must be filling before there can be pouring out; and if there is filling, there *must* be pouring out, for He hath said, *"Out of the abundance of the heart the mouth speaketh."*

But I think we should look for something more direct and definite than this. We are not all called to be the King's ambassadors, but all who have heard the messages of salvation for themselves are called to be *"the Lord's messengers,"* and day by day, as He gives us opportunity, we are to deliver *"the Lord's message, unto the people."* That message, as committed to Haggai, was, *"I am with you, saith the Lord."* Is there not work enough for any lifetime in unfolding and distributing that one message to His own people? Then, for those who are still far off, we have that equally full message from our Lord to give out, which He has condensed for us into the one word — *"Come!"*

It is an especially sweet part of His dealings with His messengers that He always gives us the message for ourselves first. It is what He has first told us in darkness — that is, in the secrecy of our own rooms, or at least of our own hearts — that He bids us speak in light. And so the more we sit at His feet and watch to see what He has to say to ourselves, the more we shall have to tell to others. He does not send us out with sealed dispatches, which we know nothing about, and with which we have no concern.

There seems a seven-fold sequence in His filling the lips of His messengers. First, they must be purified. The live coal from off the altar must be laid upon them, and He must say, *"Lo, this hath touched thy lips, and thine iniquity is taken away, and thy sin is purged."* Then He will create the fruit of them, and this seems to be the great message of peace, *"Peace to him that is far off, and to him that is near, saith the Lord; and I will heal him"* (see Isaiah 56:19). Then comes the prayer, *"O Lord, open Thou my lips,"* and its sure fulfillment. For then come in the promises, *"Behold, I have put My words in thy mouth,"* and, *"They shall* withal be fitted in thy lips." Then, of course, *"the lips of the righteous feed many,"* for the food is the Lord's own giving.

Everything leads up to praise, and so we come next to *"My mouth shall praise Thee with joyful lips, when I remember Thee."* And lest we should fancy that *'when'* rather implies that it is not, or cannot be, exactly *always*, we find that the mediation of Jesus throws this added light upon it, *"By <u>Him</u>, therefore, let us offer the sacrifice of praise to God continually, that is, the fruit of our lips, giving thanks to [confessing] His name."*

Does it seem a coming down from the mount to glance at one of our King's commandments, which is specially needful and applicable to this matter of our lips being kept for Him? *"Watch and pray, that ye enter not into temptation."* None of His commands clash with or supersede one another. Trusting does not supersede watching; it does but complete and effectuate it Unwatchful trust is a delusion, and untrustful watching is in vain. Therefore, let us not either wilfully or carelessly *enter* into temptation, whether of place, or person, or topic, which has any tendency to endanger the keeping of our lips for Jesus. Let us pray that grace may be more and more poured into our lips as it was into His, so that our speech may be *always* with grace. May they be pure, and sweet, and lovely, even as His lips, like lilies, dropping sweet-smelling myrrh.

We can hardly consider the keeping of our lips without recollecting that upon them, more than all else (though not exclusively of all else), depends that greatest of our responsibilities, our influence. We have no choice in the matter; we cannot evade or avoid it; and there is no more possibility of our limiting it, or even tracing its limits, than there is of setting a bound to the far-vibrating soundwaves, or watching their flow through the invisible air. Not one sentence that passes these lips of ours but must be an invisibly prolonged influence, not dying away into silence, but living away into the words and deeds of others. The thought would not be quite so oppressive if we could know what we have done and shall be continuing to do by what we have said. But we *never* can, as a matter of fact We may trace it a little way, and get a glimpse of some results for good or evil; but we never can see any more of it than we can see of a shooting star flashing through the night with a momentary revelation of one step of its strange path. Even if the next instant plunges it into apparent annihilation as it strikes the atmosphere of the earth, we know that it is not really so, but that its mysterious material and force must be added to the complicated materials and forces with which it has come in contact, with a modifying power none the less real because it is beyond our ken. And this is not comparing a great thing with a small, but a small thing with a great. For what is material force compared with moral force? What are gases, and vapours, and elements, compared with souls and the eternity for which they are preparing?

We all know that there is influence exerted by a person's mere presence, without the utterance of a single word. We are conscious of this every day. People seem to carry an atmosphere with them, which *must* be breathed by those whom they approach. Some carry an atmosphere in which all unkind thoughts shrivel up and cannot grow into expression. Others carry one in which *"thoughts of Christ and things divine"* never seem able to flourish. Have you not felt how a happy conversation about the things we love best is checked, or even strangled, by the entrance of one who is not in sympathy? Outsiders have not a chance of ever really knowing what delightful intercourse we have one with another about these things, because their very presence chills and changes it. On the other hand, how another person's incoming freshens and develops it and warms us all up, and seems to give us, without the least conscious effort, a sort of *lift*!

If even unconscious and involuntary influence is such a power, how much greater must it be when the recognized power of words is added!

It has often struck me as a matter of observation, that open profession adds force to this influence, on whichever side it weighs; and also, that it has the effect of making many a word and act, which might in other hands have been as nearly neutral as anything can be, tell with by no means neutral tendency on the wrong side. The question of Eliphaz comes with great force when applied to one who desires or professes to be consecrated altogether, life and lips: *"Should he reason with unprofitable talk, and with speeches <u>wherewith one can do no good</u>?"* There is our standard! Idle words, which might have fallen comparatively harmlessly from one who had never named the Name of Christ, may be a stumbling-block to inquirers, a sanction to thoughtless juniors, and a grief to thoughtful seniors, when they come from lips which are professing to feed many. Even intelligent talk on general subjects by such a one may be a chilling disappointment to some craving heart, which had indulged the hope of getting help, comfort, or instruction in the things of God by listening to the conversation. It may be a lost opportunity of giving and gaining no one knows *how* much!

How well I recollect this disappointment to myself, again and again, when a mere child! In those early seeking days, I never could understand why, sometimes, a good man whom I heard preach or speak as if he loved Christ very much, talked about all sorts of other things when he came back from church or missionary meeting. I did so wish he would have talked about the Saviour, whom I wanted, but had not round. It would have been so much more interesting even to the apparently thoughtless and merry little girl. How could he help it, I wondered, if he cared for that Pearl of Great Price as I was sure I should care for it if I could only find it! And oh, why didn't they ever talk to me about it, instead of about my lessons or their little girls at home? They did not know how their conversation was observed and compared with their sermon or speech, and how a hungry little soul went empty away from the supper table.

The lips of younger Christians may cause, in their turn, no less disappointment One sorrowful lesson I can never forget; and I will tell the story in hope that it may save others from causes of similar regret During a summer visit just after I had left school, a class of girls about my own age came to me a few times for an hour's singing. It was very pleasant indeed, and the girls were delighted with the hymns. They listened to all I had to say about time and expression, and not with less attention to the more shyly-ventured remarks about the words.

Sometimes I accompanied them afterwards down the avenue; and whenever I met any of them, I had smiles and plenty of kindly words for each, which they seemed to appreciate immensely. A few years afterwards I sat by the bedside of one of these girls — the most gifted of them all with both heart and head. She had been led by a wonderful way, and through long and deep suffering, into far clearer light than I enjoyed, and had witnessed for Christ in more ways than one, and far more brightly than I had ever done. She told me how sorrowfully and eagerly she was seeking Jesus at the time of those singing classes. And I never knew it, because I never asked, and she was too shy to speak first! But she told me more, and every word was a pang to me, — how she used to linger in the avenue on those summer evenings, longing that I would speak to her about the Saviour; how she hoped, week after week, that I would just stretch out a hand to help her, just say one little word that might be God's message of peace to her, instead of the pleasant, general remarks about the nice hymns and tunes. And I never did! And she went on for months, I think for years, after, without the light and gladness which it might have been my privilege to bring to her life. God chose other means, for the souls that He has given to Christ cannot be lost because of the unfaithfulness of a human instrument. But she said, and the words often ring in my ears when I am tempted to let an opportunity slip, *"Ah, Miss Frances, I ought to have been yours!"*

Yes, it is true enough that we should show forth His praise not only with our lips, but in our lives; but with very many Christians the other side of the prayer wants praying — they want rousing up even to wish to show it forth not only in their lives but with their lips. I wonder how many, even of those who read this, really pray, *"O Lord, open Thou my lips, and my mouth shall show forth Thy praise."*

And when opened, oh, how much one does want to have them so kept for Jesus that He may be free to make the most of them, not letting them render second-rate and indirect service when they might be doing direct and first-rate service to His cause and kingdom! It is terrible how much less is done for Him than might be done, in consequence of the specious notion that if what we are doing or saying is not bad, we are doing good in a certain way, and therefore may be quite easy about it. We should think a man rather foolish if he went on doing work which earned five shillings a week, when he might just as well do work in the same establishment and under the same master which would bring him in five pounds a week. But we should pronounce him shamefully dishonest and dishonourable if he accepted such handsome wages as the five pounds, and yet chose to do work worth only five shillings, excusing himself by saying that it was work all the same, and somebody had better do it.

Do we not act something like this when we take the lower standard; and spend our strength in just making ourselves agreeable and pleasant, creating a general good impression in favour of religion, showing that we can be all things to all men, and that one who is supposed to be a citizen of the other world can be very well up in all that concerns this world! This may be good, but is there nothing better? What does it profit if we do make this favourable impression on an outsider, if we go no farther and do not use the influence gained to bring him right inside the fold, inside the only ark of safety? People are not converted by this sort of work; at any rate, I never met or heard of anyone.

"He thinks it better for his quiet influence to tell!" said an affectionately excusing relative of one who had plenty of special opportunities of soul-winning — if he had only used his lips as well as his life for his Master.

"And how many souls have been converted to God by his 'quiet influence' all these years?" was my reply. And to that there was no answer! For the silent shining was all very beautiful in theory, but not one of the many souls placed specially under his influence had been known to be brought out of darkness into

marvellous light If they had, they must have been known, for such light can't help being seen.

When one has even a glimmer of the tremendous difference between having Christ and being without Christ; when one gets but one shuddering glimpse of what eternity is, and of what it must mean without Christ — when one gets but a flash of realization of the tremendous fact that *all* these neighbours of ours, rich and poor alike, will *have* to spend that eternity either with Him or without Him — it is hard, very hard indeed, to understand how a man or woman can believe these things at an, and make no effort for anything beyond the temporal elevation of those around, sometimes not even beyond their amusements!

"*People must have entertainment,*" they urge. I do not find that must in the Bible, but I do find, "*We must all stand before the judgment-seat of Christ*" And if you have any sort of belief in that, how can you care to use those lips of yours, which might be a fountain of life to the dying souls before you, merely to "*entertain*" them at your penny reading or other entertainment?

As you sow, so you reap. The amusing paper is read, or the lively ballad recited, or the popular song sung, and you reap your harvest of laughter or applause, and of complacence at your success in "*entertaining*" the people. And there it ends, when you might have sown words from which you and they should reap fruit unto life eternal. Is this worthy work for one who has been bought with such a price that he must say, "*Love so amazing, so divine, Demands my soul, my life, my all*"?

So far from yielding "*all*" to that rightful demand of amazing love, he does not even yield the fruit of his lips to it, much less the lips themselves. I cannot refrain from adding, that even this lower aim of "*entertaining*" is by no means so appreciated as is supposed. As a cottager of no more than average sense and intelligence remarked, *"It was all so <u>trifling</u> at the reading; I wish gentlefolks would believe that poor people like something better than what's just to make them laugh."* After all, nothing really pays like direct, straightforward, uncompromising words about God and His works and word. Nothing else ever made a man say, as a poor Irishman did when he heard the Good News for the first time, *"Thank ye, sir; you've taken the hunger off us today!"*

Jephthah uttered all his words before the Lord; what about ours? Well, they are all uttered before the Lord in one sense, whether we will or no; for *"there is not a word in my tongue, but lo, Thou, O Lord, knowest it altogether!"* How solemn is this thought, but how sweet does it become when our words are uttered consciously before the Lord as we walk in the light of His perpetual presence!

Bearing in mind that it is not only the words which pass their lightly-hinged portal, but our literal lips which are to be kept for Jesus, it cannot be out of place, before closing this chapter, to suggest that they open both ways. What passes in should surely be considered as well as what passes out. And very many of us are beginning to see that the command, *"Whether ye eat or drink, or whatsoever ye do, do all to the glory of God,"* is not fully obeyed when we drink, merely because we like it, what is the very greatest obstacle to that glory in this realm of England.

What matter that we prefer taking it in a more refined form, if the thing itself is daily and actively and mightily working misery, and crime, and death, and destruction to thousands, till the cry thereof seems as if it must pierce the very heavens! And so it does—sooner, a great deal, than it pierces the walls of our comfortable dining-room! I only say here, you who have said, *"Take my lips,"* stop and repeat that prayer next time you put that to your lips which is binding men and women hand and foot, and delivering them over, helpless, to Satan! Let those words pass once more from your heart out through your lips, and I do not think you will feel comfortable in letting the means of such infernal work pass *in* through them.

Pondering Points
BY KATIE GARRAWAY

God's Word reveals in Proverbs 18:21 that "death and life are in the power of the tongue." When you open your lips to speak throughout each day, what kind of words come out of your mouth? Kind words? Considerate words? Compassionate words? Christ-like words? Or cutting words? Cruel words? Critical words? Curse words? Again Ephesians 4:29 teaches, "Let no corrupt communication proceed out of your mouth, but that which is good to the use of edifying, that it may minister grace unto the hearers." Daily, we should pursue only the words that give grace and avoid anything idle, obscene, corrupting, offensive, and words that would stain our Christian witness.

Our words should bless and help those who hear them, not burn and hurt them. Do you need to let Jesus have control of this area of your life? God's Word rebukes in James 3:10, "Out of the same mouth proceedeth blessing and cursing. My brethren, these things ought not so to be." Our lips (which are simply the doors to the tongue) cannot be tamed without the power of God. We must give these parts of us to the Lord for Him to "keep" in control before they hurt us or others.

A sobering thought is that one day we will have to stand before God and give an account for every idle word we speak. Jesus warns us of this in Matthew 12:36-37, "But I say unto you, that every idle word that men shall speak, they shall give account thereof in the day of judgment. For by thy words thou shalt be justified, and by thy words thou shalt be condemned." Are you ready for this? If you lived with this in mind, would it help you be more careful about what you say and how you say it?

Furthermore, do your lips "show forth" the praise of God? When the unsaved are talking with you, can they tell by how you talk and what you talk about that you are a child of God? Are you always looking for a chance to bring Spiritual things into the conversation or are your lips self-centered and world-focused? May we live by the heart cry of Psalm 19:14 — "Let the words of my mouth, and the meditation of my heart, be acceptable in thy sight, O LORD, my strength, and my redeemer."

CHAPTER 7
Our Silver & Gold Kept For Jesus

*"Keep my silver and my gold;
Not a mile would I withhold."*

"The silver and the gold is Mine, saith the Lord of Hosts" (Haggai 2:8). Yes, every coin we have is literally our *"Lord's money."* Simple belief of this fact is the stepping-stone to full consecration of what He has given us, whether much or little.

"Then you mean to say we are never to spend anything on ourselves?" Not so. Another fact must be considered — the fact that our Lord has given us our bodies as a special personal charge, and that we are responsible for keeping these bodies, according to the means given and the work required, in working order for Him. This is part of our own work. A master entrusts a workman with a delicate machine, with which his appointed work is to be done. He also provides him with a sum of money with which he is to procure all that may be necessary for keeping the machine in thorough repair. Is it not obvious that it is the man's distinct duty to see to this faithfully? Would he not be

failing in duty if he chose to spend it all on something or somebody else's work, or on a present for his master, fancying that would please him better, while the machine is creaking and wearing for want of a little oil, or working badly for want of a new band or screw?

Just so, we are to spend what is really needful on ourselves, because it is our charge to do so; but not *for* ourselves, because we are not our own, but our Master's. He who *"knoweth our frame"*, knows its needs of rest and medicine, food and clothing; and the procuring of these for our own entrusted bodies should be done just as much for Jesus as the greater pleasure of procuring them for someone else.

Therefore, there need be no quibbling over the assertion that consecration is not real and complete while we are looking upon a single shilling as our own to do what we like with. Also, the principle is exactly the same, whether we are spending pence or pounds; it is our Lord's money and must not be spent without reference to Him.

When we have asked Him to take, and continually trust Him to keep our money, *"shopping"* becomes a different thing. We look up to our Lord for guidance to lay out His money prudently and rightly, and as He would have us lay it out. The gift or garment is selected consciously under His eye, and with conscious reference to Him as our own dear Master, for whose sake we shall give it, or in whose service we shall wear it, and whose own silver or gold we shall pay for it, and then it is all right.

But have you found out that it is one of the secrets of the Lord, that when any of His dear children turn aside a little bit after having once entered the blessed path of true and conscious consecration, He is sure to send them some little punishment? He will not let us go back without a sharp, even if quite secret, reminder. Go and spend ever such a little without reference to Him after you have once pledged the silver and gold entirely to Him, and see if you are not in some way rebuked for it! Very often by being permitted to find that you have made a mistake in your purchase, or that in some way it does not prosper.

If you observe these things, you will find that the more closely we are walking with our Lord, the more immediate and unmistakeable will be His gracious rebukes when we swerve in any detail of the full consecration to which He has called us. And if you have already experienced and recognised this part of His personal dealing with us, you will know also how we love and bless Him for it!

There is always a danger that just because we say *"all,"* we may practically fall shorter than if we had only said *"some,"* but said it very definitely. God recognises this and provides against it in many departments. For instance, though our time is to be all for Him, yet He solemnly sets apart the one day in seven which is to be specially for Him. Those who think they know better than God, and profess that every day is a Sabbath, little know what floodgates of temptation they are opening by being so very wise above what is written. God knows best, and that should be quite enough for every loyal heart.

So, as to money, though we place it all at our Lord's disposal, and rejoice to spend it all for Him directly or indirectly, yet I am quite certain it is a great help and safeguard, and, what is more, a matter of simple obedience to the spirit of His commands — to set aside a definite and regular proportion of our income or receipts for His direct service. It is a great mistake to suppose that the law of giving the tenth to God is merely Levitical. Search and look for yourselves, and you will find that it is, like the Sabbath, a far older rule, running all through the Bible, and endorsed, not abrogated, by Christ Himself. (See Genesis 14:20, 28:22; Leviticus 27:30 & 32; Numbers 18:21; Deuteronomy 14:22; II Chronicles 31:5, 6, 12; Nehemiah 10:37, 12:44, 13:12; Malachi 3:8 & 10; Matthew 23:23; Luke 11:42; I Corinthians 16:2; Hebrews 7:8.) For, speaking of tithes, He said, *"These ought ye to have done, and not to leave the other undone."* To dedicate the tenth of whatever we have is mere duty; charity begins beyond it; free-will offerings and thank-offerings beyond that again.

First-fruits, also, should be thus specially set apart. This, too, we find running all through the Bible. There is a tacit appeal to our gratitude in the suggestion of them — the very word implies bounty received and bounty in prospect. Bringing *"the first of the first-fruits into the house of the Lord thy God,"* was like "saying grace" for all the plenty He was going to bestow on the faithful Israelite. Something of gladness, too, seems always implied. *"The day of the first-fruits"* was to be a day of rejoicing (compare Numbers 28:26 with Deuteronomy 16:10-11). There is also an appeal to loyalty — we are commanded to *honour* the Lord with the first-fruits of all our increase. And that is the way to prosper, for the next word is, *"So shall thy barns be filled with plenty"* (Proverbs 3:9).

The friend who first called my attention to this command, said that the setting apart of first-fruits is making a proportion for God's work a first charge upon the income. This always brings a blessing on the rest, and that since this had been systematically done, the remaining funds actually seemed to go farther than expected and not thus lessened.

Presenting our first-fruits should be a peculiarly delightful act, as they are themselves the emblem of our consecrated relationship to God. For of His own will begat He us by the word of truth, that we should be a kind of first-fruits of His creatures. How sweet and hallowed and richly emblematic our little acts of obedience in this matter become, when we throw this light upon them! And how blessedly they may remind us of the heavenly company, singing, as it were, a new song before the throne; for they are the first-fruits unto God and to the Lamb.

Perhaps we shall find no better plan of detailed and systematic setting apart than the New Testament one: *"Upon the first day of the week let every one of you lay by him in store, as God hath prospered him"* (I Corinthians 16:2). The very act of literally fulfilling this apostolic command seems to bring a blessing with it, as all simple obedience. does. I wish, dear friends, you would try it! You will find it a sweet reminder on His own day of this part of your consecration. You will find it an immense help in making the most of your little charities.

The regular inflow will guide the outflow, and ensure your always having something for any sudden call for your Master's poor or your Master's cause. Do not say you are afraid you could not keep to it' What has a consecrated life to do with being 'afraid'? Some of us could tell of such sweet and singular lessons of trust in this matter, that they are written in golden letters of love on our memories. Of course there will be trials of our faith in this, as well as in everything else. But every trial of our faith is but a trial of His faithfulness, and is *"much more precious than gold which perisheth."*

"What about self-denial?" some reader will say. Consecration does not supersede this but transfigures it.

Literally, a consecrated life is and must be a life of denial of self. But all the effort and pain of it is changed into very delight We love our Master; we know, surely and absolutely, that He is listening and watching our every word and way, and that He has called us to the privilege of walking *"worthy of the Lord unto all pleasing."* And in so far as this is a reality to us, the identical things which are still self-denial in one sense, become actual self-delight in another.

It may be self-denial to us to turn away from something within reach of our purse which it would be very convenient or pleasant to possess. But if the Master lifted the veil, and revealed Himself standing at our side, and let us hear His audible voice asking us to reserve the price of it for His treasury, should we talk about self-denial then? Should we not be utterly ashamed to think of it? or rather, should we, for one instant, think about self or self-denial at all? Would it not be an unimaginable joy to do what He asked us to do with that money? But as long as His own unchangeable promise stands written in His word for us, *"Lo, I am with you alway,"* we may be sure that He is with us, and that His eye is as certainly on our opened or half-opened purse as it was on the treasury, when He sat over against it and saw the two mites cast in. So let us do our shopping *"as seeing Him who is invisible."*

It is important to remember that there is no "much or little" in God's sight, except as relatively to our means and willingness. *"For if there be first a willing mind, it is accepted according to that a man hath, and not according to that he hath not."* He knows what we *have* not, as well as what we have. He knows all about the low wages in one sphere, and the small allowance, or the fixed income with rising prices in another. And it is not a question of paying to God what can be screwed out of these, but of giving Him all, and then holding all at His disposal, and taking His orders about the disposal of all.

But I do not see at all how self-indulgence and needless extravagance can possibly co-exist with true consecration. If we really never do *go without* anything for the Lord's sake, but, just because He has graciously given us means, always supply for ourselves not only every need but every notion, I think it is high time we looked into the matter before God. Why should only those who have limited means have the privilege of offering to their Lord that which has really cost them something to offer?

Observe, it is not *merely* going without something we would naturally like to have or do, but going without it *for Jesus'* sake. Not, *"I will go without it, because, after all, I can't very well afford it;"* or, *"because I really ought to subscribe to so and so;"* or, *"because I daresay I shall be glad I have not spent the money:"* but, *"I will do without it, because I do want to do a little more for Him who so loves me — just that much more than I could do if I did this other thing."*

I fancy this is more often the heart language of those who *have* to cut and contrive, than of those who are able to give liberally without any cutting and contriving at all. The very abundance of God's good gifts too often hinders from the privilege and delight of really doing without something superfluous or comfortable or usual, that they may give just that much more to their Lord What a pity!

May what I am about to say touch someone's conscience (I pray that it will) . . . A gentleman once told us that his wine bill was £100 a year (more than enough to keep a Scripture reader always at work in some populous district). And it is one of the countless advantages of total abstinence that it at once sets free a certain amount of money for such work. Smoking, too, is a habit not only injurious to the health in a vast majority of cases, and, to our mind, very unbecoming in a 'temple of the Holy Ghost,' but also one which squanders money which might be used for the Lord. Expenses in dress might in most people be curtailed; expensive tastes should be denied; and simplicity in all habits of life should be a mark of the followers of Him who had not where to lay His head.

Truly — the self-indulgence of wealthy Christians (who might largely support the Lord's work with what they lavish upon their houses, their tables, or their personal expenditure) is very sad to see.

Here the question of jewelry seems to come in. Perhaps it was an instance of the gradual showing of the details of consecration, but I will confess that when I wrote, *"Take my silver and my gold,"* it never dawned on me that anything was included beyond the coin of the realm! But the Lord leads on softly, and a good many of us have been shown some capital bits of unenclosed but easily enclosable ground, which have yielded "pleasant fruit." Yes, very pleasant fruit! It is wonderfully nice to light upon something that we really never thought of as a possible gift to our Lord, and just to give it, straight away, to Him. I do not press the matter, but I do ask my lady friends to give it fair and candid and prayerful consideration. Which do you really care most about — a diamond on your finger, or a star in the Redeemer's kingdom, shining forever and ever? That is what it comes to, and there I leave it.

On the other hand, it is very possible to be fairly faithful in much, and yet unfaithful in that which is least. We may have thought about our gold and silver, and yet have been altogether thoughtless about our rubbish! Some have a habit of hoarding away old garments, pieces, remnants, and odds and ends generally, under the idea that they *"will come in useful some day"*; very likely setting it up as a kind of mild virtue, backed by that noxious old saying, *"Keep it by you seven years, and you'll find a use for it."* And so the shabby things get shabbier, and moth and dust doth corrupt, and the drawers and places get choked and crowded — and meanwhile all this that is sheer rubbish to you might be made useful at once (to a degree beyond what you would guess) to some poor person.

It would be a nice variety for the clever fingers of a lady's maid to be set to work to do up old things; or some tidy woman may be found in almost every locality who knows how to contrive children's things out of what seems to you only fit for the rag-bag, either for her own little ones or those of her neighbours.

My sister trimmed seventy or eighty hats every spring for several years with the contents of friends' rubbish drawers, thus relieving dozens of poor mothers who liked their children to "go tidy on Sunday," and also keeping down finery in her Sunday school. Those who literally fulfilled her request for "rubbish" used to marvel at the results.

Little scraps of carpet, torn old curtains, faded blinds, and all such gear, go a wonderfully long way towards making poor cottagers and old or sick people comfortable. I never saw anything in this "rubbish" line yet that could not be turned to good account somehow, with a little *considering* of the poor and their discomforts.

I wish my lady reader would just leave this book now and go straight up-stairs and have a good rummage at once — and see what can be thus cleared out. If she does not know the right recipients at first hand, let her send it off to the nearest working pastor's wife, and see how gratefully it will be received! For it is a great trial to workers among the poor not to be able to supply the needs they see. Such supplies are far more useful than treble their small money value.

Just a word of earnest pleading for needs, closely veiled, but very sore, which might be wonderfully lightened if this wardrobe over-hauling were systematic and faithful. There are hundreds of poor ministry families to whom a few old garments or any household oddments are as great a charity as to any of the poor under their charge. I ask my lady friends to find out how they could be a blessing to a pastor, missionary, or evangelist's family. Many struggle more than what you can see or what you will ever know. If your hearts are not so touched by their lives of brave sacrifice and many needs, then you are colder and harder than I give you credit for. Go forthwith to your wardrobes, drawers, and jewelry cabinets to see what can be spared and sent!

There is no bondage in consecration. The two things are opposites, and cannot co-exist, much less mingle. We should suspect our consecration would bring this, and then come away afresh from our great Counsellor. As long as we have an unacknowledged feeling of fidget about our account-book, and a smothered wondering what and how much we *ought* to give, and a hushed-up wishing the thing had not been put quite so strongly before us (depending upon whether or not we have said unreservedly, *"Take my silver and my gold"*). How can the Lord *keep* what He has not been sincerely asked to *take*?

Ah! if we had stood at the foot of the Cross, and watched the tremendous payment of our redemption with the precious blood of Christ! If we had seen that awful price told out, drop by drop, from His own dear patient brow and torn hands and feet, till it was ALL paid with the central word of eternity being uttered — *"It is finished!"* — should we not have been ready to say, *"Not a mile will I withhold!"*

> *Shall I hold them back — my jewels?*
> *Time has travelled many a day*
> *Since I laid them by forever,*
> *Safely locking them away;*
> *And I thought them yielded wholly,*
> *When I dared no longer wear*
> *Gems contrasting, oh, so sadly!*
> *With the adorning I would bear.*
>
> *Shall I keep them still — my jewels?*
> *Shall I, can I yet withhold*
> *From that living, loving Saviour*
> *Aught of silver or of gold?*
> *Gold so needed, that His gospel*
> *May resound from sea to sea;*
> *Can I know Christ's service lacketh,*
> *Yet forget His "unto Me"!*
>
> *No; I lay them down — my jewels,*
> *Truly on the altar now.*
> *Stay! I see a vision passing*
> *Of a gem-encircled brow:*
> *Heavenly treasure worn by Jesus,*
> *Souls won through my gift outpoured;*
> *Freely, gladly I will offer*
> *Jewels thus to crown my Lord!*

Pondering Points
BY KATIE GARRAWAY

Finances and giving to God can be a sensitive subject.
Usually, it is touchy when people remain unyielding in this area of their lives. With a white-knuckled grasp, they clench even tighter when the topic is brought up and pride mentally lashes out for the preacher to "keep his nose out of my business!" Have you surrendered this area of your life over to the Lord? Does He have access to every penny that you have to your name? He should.

Revelation 5:12 declares, "Worthy is the Lamb that was slain to receive . . . riches, . . ." When you stop and realize who Jesus is in all His omnipotent majesty and what He has so wondrously done for us through eternal salvation and even providing our "daily bread" — it should be obvious to us that He is truly the only One worthy to receive our riches. I am not worthy. You are not worthy. The world is not worthy. Sin is not worthy. Only Jesus! The word "riches" means "the multitude of my possessions, my full abundance and wealth"; it even implies to give Him "that with which I have been enriched by" — such as a career or an education. This is why so many have willingly given up a career or turned their back on a lifetime of education when God called them into full-time ministry. They realized that Jesus was worthy to receive from them even the very thing that they were being enriched by.

This mindset is hard for most American Christians today. Even missionary Jim Elliot observed this in his generation and wrote in his diary, "American believers have sold their lives to the service of Mammon, and the tombs themselves are not colder than our well-fed churches. Their condemnation is written in the dust on their Bible covers . . ."

Jesus deserves to "take" and "keep" our silver and gold because our wealth came from Him in the first place. "But thou shalt remember the LORD thy God: for it is he that giveth thee power to get wealth" (Deuteronomy 8:18). "Every man also to whom God hath given riches and wealth, and hath given him power to eat thereof, and to take his portion, and to rejoice in his labour; this is the gift of God" (Ecclesiastes 5:19).

We must be careful with money because I Timothy 6:10 warns us that ". . . the love of money is the root of all evil: which while some coveted after, they have erred from the faith, and pierced themselves through with many sorrows." The love of money is a gateway into deeper, darker sins, and will even cause a Christian to turn away from passionately living for God, leaving him with grief and regret in the end.

The purpose of life is not to make money. Proverbs 23:4-5 — "Labour not to be rich: cease from thine own wisdom. Wilt thou set thine eyes upon that which is not? For riches certainly make themselves wings; They fly away as an eagle toward heaven."

The purpose of life is to reach the world with the Gospel, fulfilling the Great Commission. The funds that we receive should be wisely stewarded so that much can be done in fulfilling the purpose for why we have been left here. Matthew 6:19-21 — "Lay not up for yourselves treasures upon earth, where moth and rust doth corrupt, and where thieves break through and steal: But lay up for yourselves treasures in heaven, where neither moth nor rust doth corrupt, and where thieves do not break through nor steal: For where your treasure is, there will your heart be also."

We must ask ourselves a very serious question — Am I robbing God? The children of Israel found this same question offensive. "Wherein have we robbed thee?" they bluntly asked the Lord with a skeptical, scoffing attitude. "In tithes and offerings," God replied. "Ye are cursed with a curse: for ye have robbed me, even this whole nation. Bring ye all the tithes into the storehouse, that there may be meat in mine house, and prove me now herewith, saith the LORD of hosts, if I will not open you the windows of heaven, and pour you out a blessing, that there shall not be room enough to receive it" (Malachi 3:8-10). Do you tithe (or give 10% of your income) to the Lord and His work? Are you looking for ways to give in special offerings to help fulfill needs of eternal significance?

Do you make sacrifices and are you willing to go without so you can give more to the Lord's work and the furtherance of the Gospel? Do you look at giving as a privilege? Or do you find yourself simply skimming from the excess? The Bible teaches us to give generously and liberally whenever the Lord directs our hearts to do so (II Corinthians 9:6-8). Be willing to give anything and everything for His kingdom!

CHAPTER 8
Our Intellects Kept For Jesus

*"Keep my intellect, and use
Every power as Thou shalt choose."*

There are two distinct sets of temptations which assail those who have, or think they have, rather less, and those who have, or think they have, rather more than an average share of intellect; while those who have neither less nor more are generally open in some degree to both. The refuge and very present help from both is the same. The intellect, whether great or small, which is committed to the Lord's keeping, will be kept and will be used by Him.

The former class are tempted to think themselves excused from effort to cultivate and use their small intellectual gifts; to suppose they cannot or need not seek to win souls, because they are not so clever and apt in speech as So-and-so; to attribute to want of gift what is really want of grace; to hide the one talent because it is not five. Let me throw out a thought or two for these.

Which is greatest, gifts or grace? *Gifts* are given *"to every man according to his severability."* That is, we have just as much given as God knows we are able to use, and what He knows we can best use for Him. *"But unto every one of us is given grace according to the measure of the gift of Christ."* Claiming and using that royal measure of grace, you may, and can, and will do more for God than the mightiest intellect in the world without it For which, in the clear light of His Word, is likely to be most effectual, the natural ability which at its best and fullest, without Christ, *"can do nothing"* (observe and believe that word!), or the grace of our Almighty God and the power of the Holy Ghost; which is as free to you as it ever was to anyone?

If you are responsible for making use of your limited gift, are you not equally responsible for making use of the grace and power which are to be had for the asking, which are already yours in Christ, and which are not limited?

Also, do you not see that when there are great natural gifts, people give the credit to *them*, instead of to the grace which alone did the real work, and thus God is defrauded of the glory? So that, to say it reverently, God can get more glory out of a feeble instrument, because then it is more obvious that the excellency of the power is of God and not of us. Will you not henceforth say, *"Most gladly, therefore, will I rather glory in my infirmities, that the power of Christ may rest upon me"*?

Don't you really believe that the Holy Spirit is just as able to draw a soul to Jesus, if He will, by your whisper of the one word *"Come,"* as by an eloquent sermon an hour long? *I* do! At the same time, as it is evidently God's way to work through these intellects of ours, we have no more right to expect Him to use a mind which we are wilfully neglecting, and taking no pains whatever to fit for His use, than I should have to expect you to write a beautiful inscription with my pen, if I would not take the trouble to wipe it and mend it.

The latter class are tempted to rely on their natural gifts, and to act and speak in their own strength; to go on too fast, without really looking up at every step, and for every word; to spend their Lord's time in polishing up their intellects, nominally for the sake of influence and power, and so forth, while really, down at the bottom, it is for the sake of the keen enjoyment of the process; and perhaps, most of all, to spend the strength of these intellects *"for that which doth not profit,"* in yielding to the specious snare of reading clever books on both "sides", and eating deliberately of the tree of the knowledge of good *and evil*.

The mere mention of these temptations should be sufficient appeal to conscience. If consecration is to be a reality anywhere, should it not be in the very thing which you own as an extra gift from God, and which is evidently closest, so to speak, to His direct action, spirit upon spirit? And if the very strength of your intellect has been your weakness, will you not entreat Him to keep it henceforth really and entirely for Himself? It is so good of Him to have given you something to lay at His feet; shall not this goodness lead you to lay it all there, and never hanker after taking it back for yourself or the world? Do you not feel that in very proportion to the gift you need the special keeping of it? He may lead you by a way you know not in the matter; very likely He will show you that you must be willing to be a fool for His sake first, before He will condescend to use you much for His glory. Will you look up into His face and say, *"Not willing"*?

He who made every power can use every power — memory, judgment, imagination, quickness of apprehension or insight;

specialties of, musical, poetical, oratorical, or artistic faculty; special tastes for reasoning, philosophy, history, natural science, or natural history — all these may be dedicated to Him, sanctified by Him, and used by Him. Whatever He has given, He will use, if we will let Him. Often, in the most unexpected ways, and at the most unexpected turns, something read or acquired long ago suddenly comes into use. We cannot foresee what will thus *"come in useful"*; but He knew, when He guided us to learn it, what it would be wanted for in His service. So may we not ask Him to bring His perfect foreknowledge to bear on all our mental training and storing? To guide us to read or study exactly what He knows there will be use for in the work to which He has called or will call us?

Nothing is more practically perplexing to a young Christian, whose preparation time is not quite over, or perhaps painfully limited, than to know what is most worth studying, what is really the best investment of the golden hours, while yet the time is not come for the field of active work to be fully entered, and the *"thoroughly furnishing"* of the mind is the evident path of present duty. Is not His name called *"Counsellor"*? and will He not be faithful to the promise of His name in this, as well as in all else?

The same applies to every subsequent stage. Only let us be perfectly clear about the principle that our intellect is not our own, either to cultivate, or to use, or to enjoy, and that Jesus Christ is our real and ever-present Counsellor, and then there will be no more worry about what to read and how much to read, and whether to keep up one's accomplishments, or one's languages, or one's *"ologies"*! If the Master has need of them, He will show us; and if He has not, what need have we of them? If we go forward without His leading, we may throw away some talent, or let it get too rusty for use, which would have been most valuable when other circumstances arose or different work was given. We must not think that *"keeping"* means <u>not using at all</u>! What we want is to have all our powers kept for His *use*.

In this they will probably find far higher development than in any other sort of use. I know cases in which the effect of real consecration on mere mental development has been obvious and surprising to all around. Yet it is only a confirmation of what I believe to be a great principle, viz. that *the Lord makes the most of whatever is unreservedly surrendered to Him*. There will always be plenty of waste in what we try to cut out for ourselves. But He wastes no material!

Pondering Points
BY KATIE GARRAWAY

Which end of the spectrum do you find yourself on? Feeling intellectually inferior and using the excuse, "I don't know how to do that" to shy away from areas God may be calling you to serve in? Or do you find yourself confident in your intellectual abilities, proudly excelling in everything you put your hand to and forgetting to rely on the Spirit's power and strength? No matter which side you may find yourself on at times, remember to always turn to God and depend on His grace and power.

Always learn to give God the glory for any wisdom that you obtain, because the Bible says in Ecclesiastes 2:26 — "God giveth to a man that is good in his sight wisdom, and knowledge, and joy". Truly, we have nothing to boast of, save that which the Lord has given to us and done for us. He is the One Who gives the spirit of understanding and the mental prowess to gain knowledge in the first place.

If you lack wisdom, do not quit with a shrug of the shoulders. This is an outward sign of a mind that is not surrendered. The Bible says in James 1:5, "If any of you lack wisdom, let him ask of God, that giveth to all men liberally, and upbraideth not; and it shall be given him." It might not come easy, but any wisdom sought through the spirit of prayer may be obtained by the hand of God. Realize that He will never call upon you to learn something that cannot be done through Him.

Truly, our Lord does not deserve "I don't know" for an answer! Again, Revelation 5:12 declares, "Worthy is the Lamb that was slain to receive . . . wisdom, . . ." Jesus deserves to receive from each of us all our mind — our entire intellect.

CHAPTER 9
Our Wills Kept For Jesus

*"Keep my will, oh, keep it Thine,
For it is no longer mine."*

Perhaps there is no point in which expectation has been so limited by experience as this. We believe God is able to do for us just so much as He has already done, and no more. We take it for granted a line must be drawn somewhere; and so we choose to draw it where experience ends, and faith would have to begin.

Even if we have trusted and proved Him as to keeping our members and our minds, faith fails when we would go deeper and say, *"Keep my will!"* And yet the only reason we have to give is, that though we have asked Him to take our will, we do not exactly find that it is altogether His, but that self-will crops up again and again.

And whatever flaw there might be in this argument, we think the matter is quite settled by the fact that some whom we rightly esteem, and who are far better than ourselves, have the same experience, and do not even seem to think it right to hope for anything better. That is conclusive! And the result of this, as of every other faithless conclusion, is either discouragement and depression, or, still worse, acquiescence in an unyielded will, as something that can't be helped.

Now let us turn from our thoughts to God's thoughts. Verily, they are not as ours! He says, *"He is able to do exceeding abundantly above all that we ask or think."* Apply this here. We ask him to take our wills and make them His. Does He or does He not mean what He says? If He does, should we not trust Him to do this thing that we have asked and longed for, and not less but more? *"Is <u>anything</u> too hard for the Lord?"* *"Hath He said, and shall He not do it?"*

And if He gives us faith to believe that we have the petition that we desired of Him, and with it the unspeakable rest of leaning our will wholly upon His love, what ground have we for imagining that this is *necessarily* to be a mere fleeting shadow, which is hardly to last an hour, but is *necessarily* to be exhausted ere the next breath of trial or temptation comes? Does He mock our longing by acting as I have seen an older person act to a child, by accepting some trifling gift of no intrinsic value, just to please the little one, and then throwing it away as soon as the child's attention is diverted? Is not the taking rather the pledge of the keeping, if we will but entrust Him fearlessly with it? We give Him no opportunity, so to speak, of proving His faithfulness to this great promise, because we will not fulfill the condition of reception — believing it!

But we readily enough believe instead all that we hear of the unsatisfactory experience of others! Or, start from another word. Job said, *"I know that Thou canst do everything,"* and we turn round and say, *"Oh yes, everything <u>except</u> keeping my will!"*

Dare we add, *"And I know that Thou canst not do that"*? Yet that is what is said every day, only in other words; and if not said aloud, it is said in faithless hearts, and God hears it What does *"Almighty"* mean, if it does not mean, as we teach our little children, able to do <u>everything</u>?

We have asked this great thing many a time, without, perhaps, realizing how great a petition we were singing, in the old morning hymn, *"Guard my first springs of thought and will!"* That goes to the root of the matter, only it implies that the will has been already surrendered to Him, that it may be wholly kept and guarded.

It may be that we have not sufficiently realized the sin of the only alternative. Our wills belong either to self or to God. It may seem a small and rather excusable sin in man's sight to be self-willed, but see in what a category of iniquity God puts it! (II Peter 2:10) And certainly we are without excuse when we have such a promise to go upon as, *"It is God that worketh in you both to <u>will</u> and to do of His pleasure."* How splendidly this meets our very deepest helplessness — worketh in you to *will!* Oh, let us pray for ourselves and for each other, that we may know *"what is the exceeding greatness of His power to usward who believe."* It does not say, to usward who fear and doubt; for if we will not believe, neither shall we be established. If we will not believe what God says He can do, we shall see it with our eyes, but we shall not eat thereof. *"They <u>could</u> <u>not</u> enter in because of unbelief."*

It is most comforting to remember that the grand promise, *"Thy people shall be willing in the day of Thy power,"* is made by the Father to Christ Himself: The Lord Jesus holds this promise, and God will fulfill it to Him. He will make us willing because

He has promised Jesus that He will do so. And what is being made willing, but having our will taken and kept?

All true surrender of the will is based upon love and knowledge of, and confidence in, the one to whom it is surrendered. We have the human analogy so often before our eyes, that it is the more strange we should be so slow to own even the possibility of it as to God. Is it thought anything so very extraordinary and high-flown, when a bride deliberately *prefers* wearing a colour which was not her own taste or choice, because her husband likes to see her in it? Is it very unnatural that it is no distress to her to do what he asks her to do, or to go with him where he asks her to come, even without question or explanation, instead of doing what or going where she would undoubtedly have preferred if she did not know and love him?

Is it very surprising if this lasts beyond the wedding day, and if year after year she still finds it her greatest pleasure to please him, quite irrespective of what *used* to be her own ways and likings? Yet in this case she is not helped by any promise or power on his part to make her wish what he wishes. But He who so wonderfully condescends to call Himself the Bridegroom of His church, and who claims our fullest love and trust, has promised and has power to work in us to will. Shall we not claim His promise and rely on His mighty power, and say, not self-confidently, but looking only unto Jesus —

> *Keep my will, for it is Thine;*
> *It shall be no longer mine!*

Only in proportion as our own will is surrendered, are we able to discern the true glory of God's will.

> *For oh! it is a splendour,*
> *A glow of majesty,*
> *A mystery of beauty*
> *If we will only see;*
> *A very cloud of glory*
> *Enfolding you and me.*
>
> *A splendour that is lighted*
> *At one transcendent flame,*
> *The wondrous Love, the perfect Love,*
> *Our Father's sweetest name;*
> *For His Name and very Essence*
> *And His Will are all the same!*

Conversely, in proportion as we see this splendour of His will, we shall more readily or more fully surrender our own. Not until we have presented our bodies a living sacrifice can we prove what is that good, and perfect, and acceptable will of God. But in thus proving it, this continual presentation will be more and more seen to be our reasonable service and becomes more and more a joyful sacrifice of praise.

The connection in Romans 12:1-2, between our sacrifice which He so graciously calls acceptable to Himself, and our finding out that His will is acceptable to ourselves, is very striking. One reason for this connection may be that only love can really understand love, and love on both sides is at the bottom of the whole transaction and its results. First, He loves us. Then the discovery of this leads us to love Him. Then, because He loves us, He claims us, and desires to have us wholly yielded to His will, so that the operations of love in and for us may find no hindrance. Then, because we love Him we recognise His claim and yield ourselves. Then, being thus yielded, He draws us nearer to Him, (II Chronicles 29:31 — *"Now ye have consecrated yourselves unto the LORD, come near . . ."*) and admits us, so to speak, into closer intimacy, so that we gain nearer and truer views of His perfections. Then the unity of these perfections becomes clearer to us.

Now we not only see His justice and mercy flowing in an undivided stream from the cross of Christ, but we see that they never were divided, though the strange distortions of the dark, false glass of sin made them appear so, but that both are but emanations of God's Holy love. Then having known and believed this Holy love, we see further that His will is not a separate thing, but only love (and therefore all His attributes) in action; love being. the primary essence of His being, and all the other attributes manifestations and combinations of that ineffable essence, for God is *Love*.

Then this will of God which has seemed in old far-off days a stem and fateful power, is seen to be only love energized; love saying, *"I will."* And when once we really grasp this (hardly so much by faith as by love itself), the will of God cannot be otherwise than acceptable, for it is no longer a question of trusting that somehow or other — there is a hidden element of love in it. Understanding that it is love brings great light and warmth like the power of the sun's rays. Love recognised surely will be love accepted and love reciprocated. So, as the fancied sternness of God's will is lost in His love, the stubbornness of our will becomes melted in that love, and lost in our acceptance of it. From this, our hearts will undoubtedly cry — *"Do thine own way with me, Lord, in Thy wonderful grand will!"*

Pondering Points
BY KATIE GARRAWAY

Do you believe that God's will for your life is "good, acceptable, and perfect"? Are you convinced that His designs are far superior and will far surpass your own desires? Do you view God's will as a "Have to" or a "Get to" and "Want to"? Does your heart find great peace, joy, and satisfaction knowing that God is real and that His will for your life is real? Or do you think deep down that you can do better than God? Do you wrestle in your spirit with releasing your will into God's loving hand? Do you doubt Him? Or do you love Him with an eagerness to pursue Him? Isaiah 64:4 promises, "For since the beginning of the world men have not heard, nor perceived by the ear, neither hath the eye seen, O God, beside thee, what he hath prepared for him that waiteth for him."

Missionary Jim Elliot wrote in his diary, "Our dreams are tawdry (showy, but cheap and of poor quality) when they are compared to the leading of God. They are not worthy of the aura of wonder we usually surround them with. God only doeth wonders. His hand can work nothing less. In my own experience, I have found that the most extravagant dreams of boyhood have not surpassed the great experience of being in God's will. I believe that nothing could be better. His will is always a bigger thing than we bargained for, but we must believe that whatever it involves: it is good, acceptable, & perfect."

Truly — to seek God's will is life's greatest journey, to find God's will is life's greatest discovery, to do God's will is life's greatest accomplishment, but to ignore God's will is life's greatest tragedy. There will never be regret in the center of God's will — no matter where it leads, whether in green pastures, beside still waters, on the steady paths of righteousness, through the valley of the shadow of death, or on the rugged battlefield (Psalm 23:2-5). Anyone who has followed the Lord through it all will joyfully testify, "Surely goodness and mercy shall follow me ALL the days of my life!"

God wants you to surrender to His will, denying your own, because you know the greatness of His wonder and love. You can always trust Him completely because He always wants what's best for you!

CHAPTER 10
Our Hearts Kept For Jesus

"Keep my heart; it is Thine own;
It is now Thy royal throne."

"It is a good thing that the heart be established with grace," and yet some of us go on as if it were not a good thing even to hope for it to be so. Let me explain.

We would be ashamed to say that we had behaved treacherously to a friend; that we had played him false again and again; that we had said scores of times what we did not really mean; that we had professed and promised what, all the while, we had no sort of purpose of performing. We should be ready to go off by next ship to New Zealand rather than calmly own to all this, or rather than ever face out friends again after we had owned it. And yet we are not ashamed (some of us) to say that we are always dealing treacherously with our Lord!

Nay, more, we own it with an inexplicable complacency, as if there were a kind of virtue in saying how fickle and faithless and desperately wicked our hearts are; and we actually plume ourselves on the easy confession, which we think proves our humility. Yet this does not lower us in the eyes of others, nor in our own eyes, half so much as if we had to say, *"I have told a lie,"* or, *"I have broken my promise."* Nay, more, we have not the slightest hope, and therefore not the smallest intention of aiming at an utterly different state of things. It would be good for us if we do not go a step farther, and call those by hard and false names who do not seek to have an established heart, and who do not believe what the Lord meant when He promised, *"No good thing will He withhold from them that walk uprightly."* If so, might it be that He will withhold good things from us also?

Let us pray for Him to establish our hearts to walk uprightly. Our prayer must be based upon this promise, and, thank God, His promises are always broader than our prayers. No fear of building inverted pyramids here, for Jesus Christ is the foundation, and this and all the other *"promises of God in Him are yea, and in Him amen, unto the glory of God by us."* So it shall be unto His glory to fulfil this one to us, and to answer our prayer for a *"kept"* or *"established"* heart. And its fulfilment shall work out His glory, not in spite of us, but *"by us."*

We find both the means and the result of the keeping in the Psalm 112: *"His heart is fixed."* Whose heart? An angel? A saint in glory? No! Simply the heart of the man that *"feareth the Lord, and delighteth greatly in His commandments."* Therefore, yours and mine, as God would have them be; just the normal idea of a God-fearing heart . . . This is nothing extremely and hopelessly beyond attainment.

"Fixed." How does that tally with the deceitfulness and waywardness and fickleness about which we really talk as if we were rather proud of them than utterly ashamed of them?

Does our heavenly Bridegroom expect nothing more of us? Does His mighty, all-constraining love intend to do no more for us than to leave us in this deplorable state, when He is undoubtedly able to heal the desperately wicked heart (compare verses 9 and 14 of Jeremiah 17), to rule the wayward one with His peace, and to establish the fickle one with His grace? Are we not *"without excuse"*?

"Fixed, trusting in the Lord." Here is the means of the fixing — trust. He works the trust in us by sending the Holy Spirit to reveal God in Christ to us as absolutely, infinitely worthy of our trust When we *"see Jesus"* by Spirit-wrought faith, we cannot but trust Him; we distrust our hearts more truly than ever before, but we trust our Lord entirely, because we trust Him only. For, entrusting our trust to Him, we know that He is able to keep that which we commit (*i.e.* entrust) to Him. It is His own way of winning and fixing our hearts for Himself Is it not a beautiful one? Thus *"his heart is established."* But we have not quite faith enough to believe that. So what is the very first doubting, and therefore sad thought that crops up? *"Yes, but I am <u>afraid</u> it will not remain fixed."*

That is *your* thought. Now see what is God's thought about the case. *"His heart is established, he shall not be afraid."*

Is not that enough? What *is*, if such plain and yet divine words are not? Well, the Gracious One bears with us, and gives line upon line to His poor little children. And so He says, *"The peace of God, which passeth all understanding, shall keep your hearts and minds, through Christ Jesus."* And again, *"Thy thoughts shall be established."* And again, *"Thou wilt keep him in perfect peace, whose mind is stayed on Thee, because he trusteth in Thee."*

And to prove to us that these promises can be realized in present experience, He sends down to us through nearly 3000 years the words of the man who prayed, *"Create in me a clean heart, O God,"* and lets us bear twice over the new song put by the same Holy Spirit into his mouth: *"My heart is fixed, O God, my heart is fixed"* (Psalm 57:7 and 108:1).

The heart that is established in Christ is also established for Christ It becomes His royal throne, no longer occupied by His foe, no longer tottering and unstable. And then we see the beauty and preciousness of the promise, *"He shall be a Priest upon His throne."* Not only reigning, but atoning. Not only ruling, but cleansing. Thus the throne is established not only in mercy, but also by righteousness.

I think we lose ground sometimes by parleying with the tempter. We have no business to parley with a usurper — whether that be the flesh or the Devil. The throne is no longer either of theirs when we have surrendered it to our Lord Jesus. And why should we allow them to argue with us for one instant, as if it were still an open question? Don't listen; simply tell them that Jesus Christ *is* on the long-disputed throne and forever will be. And you will have no more about it but turn at once to your King and claim the glorious protection of His sovereignty over you. It is a splendid reality, and you will find it so. He will not abdicate and leave you kingless and defenseless. For verily, *"The Lord is our King; He will save us"* (Isaiah 33:22).

Our Hearts Are Naturally	*God Can Make Them*
Evil *(Hebrews 3:12)*	Clean *(Psalm 51:10)*
Desperately Wicked *(Jeremiah 17:9)*	Honest and Good *(Luke 8:15)*
Weak *(Ezekiel 16:30)*	Fixed *(Psalm 112:7)*
Deceitful *(Jeremiah 17:9)*	Faithful *(Nehemiah 9:8)*
Deceived *(Isaiah 44:20)*	Understanding *(I Kings 3:9)*
Double *(Psalm 12:2)*	Humble *(Isaiah 57:15)*
Impenitent *(Romans 2:5)*	Contrite *(Psalm 51:17)*
Rebellious *(Jeremiah 5:23)*	True *(Hebrews 10:22)*
Hard *(Ezekiel 3:7)*	Soft *(Job 23:16)*
Stony *(Ezekiel 11:19)*	New *(Ezekiel 18:31)*
Froward *(Proverbs 17:20)*	Sound *(Psalm 119:80)*
Despiteful *(Ezekiel 25:15)*	Glad *(Psalm 16:9)*
Stout *(Isaiah 10:12)*	Established *(Psalm 112:8)*
Haughty *(Proverbs 18:12)*	Tender *(Ephesians 4:32)*
Proud *(Proverbs 21:4)*	Pure *(Matthew 5:8)*
Perverse *(Proverbs 12:8)*	Perfect *(I Chronicles 29:9)*
Foolish *(Romans 1:21)*	Wise *(Proverbs 11:29)*

Pondering Points
BY KATIE GARRAWAY

Once you've given your heart to Christ and let Him save you, He wants to keep your heart as His throne every day of your life. Does He not deserve this? And what joy there is in knowing that He wants to be King in our hearts! Do you let Him rule and reign there? Or do you grieve Him with sin (whether secret or known), shoving Him off the throne and letting Satan or your flesh rule there instead?

One of our greatest adversaries is our flesh. We know the flesh is constantly struggling for control. We can all feel it. Every day, this battle will rage. Galatians 5:17 says, "For the flesh lusteth against the Spirit, and the Spirit against the flesh: and these are contrary the one to the other: so that ye cannot do the things that ye would." Our lustful, dictatorial flesh is a vicious adversary, hungering to yank us about in its self-willed chains and drag us down into crippling captivity. It's going to fight us tooth-and-nail, kicking and screaming! The flesh doesn't want to be controlled; it wants to be in control. The flesh doesn't want to "die to self"; it wants to dominate. It wants to bring our heart for God down into subjection unto its whims and wants. It does not want to be "crucified" as the Bible teaches. It wants to claim complete ownership over your existence and leave no room for God.

We also must be careful to not be deceived. Just because we are reading our Bibles, praying, and engaged in Christ-honoring work does not always mean that Christ is automatically sitting upon the throne of our hearts. We can easily be guilty of performing religious activities in the flesh. Check your heart. The flesh could still be in control as is a puppet master, pulling the strings from behind the scenes, causing us to lead a Pharisaical life.

Today through the person and power of Christ, arise and tell your flesh and the Devil that their time on the throne of your heart has come to an end! Relinquish it back to its rightful Owner, the One who gave His life to redeem it. Give it to King Jesus!

CHAPTER 11
Our Love Kept For Jesus

*"Keep my love; my Lord, I pour
At Thy feet its treasure-store."*

Not as a mere echo from the morning-gilded shore of Tiberias — but as an ever new, ever sounding note of divinest power — comes the familiar question to each of us, *"Lovest thou Me?"* He who says it has loved us with an everlasting love. He who says it has died for us. He who says it has washed us from our sins in His own blood. He who says it has waited for our love, waited patiently all through our coldness.

And if by His grace we have said, *"Take my love,"* which of us has not felt that part of His very answer has been to make us see how little there was to take, and how little of that little has been kept for Him? And yet we *do* love Him! He knows that! The very mourning and longing to love Him more proves it. But we should want more than that, and so does our Lord.

He has created us to love. We have a sealed treasure of love, which either remains sealed, and then gradually dries up and wastes away, or is unsealed and poured out, and yet is the fuller and not the emptier for the outpouring. The more love we give, the more we have to give. So far it is only natural. But when the Holy Spirit reveals the love of Christ, and sheds abroad the love of God in our hearts, this natural love is penetrated with a new principle, as it discovers a new Object. Everything that it beholds in that Object gives it new depth and new colours. As it sees the holiness, the beauty, and the glory, it takes the deep hues of conscious sinfulness, unworthiness, and nothingness. As it sees even a glimpse of the love that passeth knowledge, it takes the glow of wonder and gratitude. And when it sees that love drawing close to its deepest need with blood — purchased pardon, it is intensified and stirred, and there is no more time for weighing. and measuring; we must pour it out, all there is of it, with our tears, at the feet that were pierced for love of us.

And what then? Has the flow grown gradually slower and shallower? Has our Lord reason to say, *"My brethren have dealt deceitfully as a brook, and as a stream of brooks they pass away"*? It is humiliating to have found that we could not keep on loving Him, as we loved in that remembered hour when *"Thy time was the time of love."* We have proved that we were not able. Let this be only the stepping-stone to proving that He is able!

There will have been a cause, as we shall see if we seek it honestly. It was not that we really poured out all our treasure, and so it naturally came to an end. We let it be secretly diverted into other channels. We began keeping back a line part of the price for something else. We looked away from, instead of looking away unto Jesus. We did not entrust Him with our love and ask Him to keep it for Himself.

And what has He to say to us? Ah, He upbraideth not. Listen! *"Thus saith the Lord, I remember thee, the kindness of thy youth, the love of thine espousals."* Can any words be more tender, more touching, to you, to me? Forgetting all the sin, all the backsliding, all the coldness, casting all that into the unreturning depths of the sea, He says He remembers that hour when we first said, *"Take my love."* He remembers it now, at this minute. He has written it forever on His infinite memory, where the past is as the present.

His own love is unchangeable, so it could never be His wish or will that we should thus drift away from Him. Have we told Him, *"Take my love"* and then we have removed it and given it to another? Oh, *"Come and let us return unto the Lord!"* But is there any hope that, thus returning; our flickering love may be kept from again failing? Hear what He says: *"And I will betroth thee unto Me forever."* And again: *"Thou shalt abide for Me many days; so will I also be for thee."* Shall we trust His word or not? Is it worthy of our acceptation or not? Oh, rest on this word of the King, and let Him from this day have the keeping of your love, and He will keep it!

The love of Christ is not an absorbing love, but a radiating love. The more we love Him, the more we shall most certainly love others. Some have not much natural power of loving, but the love of Christ will strengthen it Some have had the springs of love dried up by some terrible earthquake. They will find "fresh springs" in Jesus and the gentle flow will be purer and deeper than the old torrent could ever be. Some have been satisfied that it should rush in a narrow channel, but He will cause it to overflow into many another and widen its course of blessing. Some have spent it all on their God-given dear ones. Now He is come whose right it is; and yet in the fullest resumption of that right, He is so gracious that He puts back an even larger measure of the old love into our hand, sanctified with His own love, and energized with His blessing, and strengthened with His new commandment, *"That ye love one another, as I have loved you."*

And a true test of our inward love for Him will be found in what He said would be the outward proof of our love: *"If ye love me, keep my commandments."* And *"For this is the love of God, that we keep his commandments: and his commandments are not grievous."* If we have allowed Him to *"keep our love"* then we will find joy and lightness in keeping His Word. You cannot love Him in word and then not in deed. (*"Let us not love in word, neither in tongue; but in deed and in truth."*) That is not a heart or life true love to our Lord.

A question has been discussed in recent days that raises a very interesting part — *"When does love become idolatry? Does the coming in of another person of affection interfere with entire consecration and affection to God?"* It seems to me that He Who is love would not give us an object for our love unless He saw that our hearts needed expansion; and if the love is consecrated, and the friendship takes its stand in Christ, there is no need for the fear that it will become idolatry. Let the love on both sides *be given to God to keep*, and however much it may grow, the Source of Christ from which it springs must yet be greater. He would have us to *"love thy neighbour."* Also, *"A new commandment I give unto you, That ye love one another; as I have loved you, that ye also love one another. By this shall all men know that ye are my disciples, if ye have love one to another."* The Lord would have us to love others as He loves us, and as our love grows, may our love for Him, Who is Love, increase without measure, full and boundless!

There is no love so deep and wide as that which is kept for Jesus. It flows both fuller and farther when it flows only through Him. Then, too, it will be a power for Him. It will always be unconsciously working for Him. In drawing others to ourselves by it, we shall be necessarily drawing them nearer to the Fountain of our love, never drawing them away from it. It is the great magnet of His love which alone can draw any heart to Him; but when our own are thoroughly yielded to its mighty influence, they will be so magnetized that He will condescend to use them in this way.

Is it not wonderful to think that the Lord Jesus will not only accept and keep our love, but actually *use* it for His glory?

Pondering Points
by KATIE GARRAWAY

How vast is the measure of your love for Jesus? Do you passionately love Him as much as He passionately loves you? Are you guilty of saying that you love Him and then not showing Him or living in such a way that proves your unwavering love for Christ? Our love for Jesus should be so intense that nothing — "tribulation, or distress, or persecution, or famine, or nakedness, or peril, or sword... death, nor life, nor angels, nor principalities, nor powers, nor things present, nor things to come, nor height, nor depth, nor any other creature, shall be able to separate us from the love of God, which is in Christ Jesus our Lord" (Romans 8:35-39).

Have you fallen out of love with Jesus and fallen in love with someone or something else? Does something or someone bring you greater joy, satisfaction, and fulfillment than Jesus? What about money, sports, apparel and appearance, entertainment, technology, cars, houses, approval of men, food, addictions, lust, "pleasures" of sin, etc? I John 2:15 declares, "Love not the world, neither the things that are in the world. If any man love the world, the love of the Father is not in him."

Everything we do should be borne out of our genuine love for Him and His love for us. II Corinthians 5:14 says, "For the love of Christ constraineth us..." Does this verse define the "why" behind the "what" and the "how" of who we are and what we do? "And thou shalt love the Lord thy God with all thy heart, and with all thy soul, and with all thy mind, and with all thy strength:" (Mark 12:30). God's love should be the central motivating factor. May another generation arise whose hearts <u>BURN</u> for Jesus — lives that are ablaze with a love and an adoration for Christ that <u>NOTHING</u> can extinguish!

When you surrender and say, "<u>Take my love</u>", you must continue to hold Him close Who ever loveth you to "<u>keep my love</u>." Only by this will you "be able to comprehend with all saints what is the breadth, and length, and depth, and height; And to know the love of Christ, which passeth knowledge, that ye might be filled with all the fulness of God" (Ephesians 3:17-19). When you fully grasp the expanse of His love for you, you will then be able to love Him more in return. And His love can flow through you to those around you. Does your heart overflow with love for others, putting them before yourself? Just as Jesus sacrificed for others and put them first, so should we.

CHAPTER 12
Our Selves Kept For Jesus

*"Keep my self, that I may be
Ever, only, all for Thee."*

"FOR THEE!" That is the beginning and the end of the whole matter of consecration.

There was a prelude to its endless song, — a prelude whose theme is woven into every following harmony in the new anthem of consecrated life: *"The Son of God, who loved me, and gave Himself for me."* Out of the realized *"for me,"* grows the practical and obvious *"for Thee!"* If the former is a living root, the latter will be its living fruit.

"For Thee!" This makes the difference between forced or formal, and therefore unreasonable service, and the *"reasonable service"* which is the beginning of the perfect service where they see His face. This makes the difference between slave work and free work. For Thee, my Redeemer; for Thee who hast spoken to my heart; for Thee, who hast done for me — *what?* Let us each pause, and fill up that blank with the great things the Lord hath

done for us. For Thee, who art to me — what? Fill that up too, before Him! **FOR THEE,** my Saviour Jesus, my Lord and God!

And what is to be for Him? *My self.* We talk sometimes as if, whatever else could be subdued unto Him, self could never be. Did Paul forget to mention this important exception to the *"all things"* in Philippians 3:21? David said: *"Bless the Lord, O my soul, and all that is within me, bless His Holy Name."* Did he, too, unaccountably forget to mention that he only meant all that was within him, except self? If not, then self must be among the *"all things"* which the Lord Jesus Christ is able to subdue unto Himself, and which are to *"bless His Holy Name."* It is Self which, once His most treacherous foe, is now, by full and glad surrender, His own soldier — coming over from the rebel camp into the royal army. It is not someone else, some temporarily possessing spirit, which says within us, *"Lord, Thou knowest that I love Thee,"* but our true and very self; only changed and renewed by the power of the Holy Ghost. And when we do that we would not, we know that *"it is no more I that do it, but sin that dwelleth in me."* Our true self is the new self, taken and won by the love of God, and kept by the power of God.

Yes, *"kept!"* There is the promise on which we ground our prayer; or, rather, one of the promises. For, search and look for your own strengthening and comfort, and you will find it repeated in every part of the Bible, from *"I am with thee, and will keep thee,"* in Genesis, to *"I also will keep thee from the hour of temptation,"* in Revelation.

And kept *for Him!* Why should it be thought a thing incredible with you, when it is only the fulfilling of His own eternal purpose in creating us? *"This people have I formed for Myself."* Not ultimately only, but presently and continually; for

He says, *"Thou shalt abide for Me;"* and, *"He that remaineth, even he shall be for our God."* Are you one of His people by faith in Jesus Christ? Then see what you are to Him. You, personally and individually, are part of the Lord's portion (Deuteronomy 32:9) and of His inheritance (I Kings 8:53 & Ephesians 1:18). His portion and inheritance would not be complete without you; you are His peculiar treasure (Exodus 19:5); *"a special people"* (how warm, and loving, and natural that expression is!) *"unto Himself"* (Deuteronomy 7:6). Would you call it *"keeping,"* if you had a special treasure, a darling little child, for instance, and let it run wild into all sorts of dangers all day long, sometimes at your side, and sometimes out in the street, with only the intention of fetching it safe home at night? If ye then, being evil, would know better, and do better, than that, how much more shall our Lord's keeping be true, and tender, and continual, and effectual, when He declares us to be His peculiar treasure, purchased (See I Peter 2:9) for Himself at such unknown cost!

> *He will keep what thus He sought,*
> *Safely guard the dearly bought;*
> *Cherish that which He did choose,*
> *Always love and never lose.*

I know what some of us are thinking. *"Yes; I see it all plainly enough in theory, but in practice I find I am not kept. Self goes over to the other camp again and again. It is not all for Jesus, though I have asked and wished for it to be so."* Dear friends, the **"all"** must be sealed with **"only."** Are you willing to be *"only"* for Jesus? You have not given *"all"* to Jesus while you are not quite ready to be, *"only"* for Him. And it is no use to talk about *"ever"* while we have not settled the *"only"* and the *"all."* You cannot be *"for Him,"* in the full and blessed sense, while you are partly for anything or anyone else. For *"the Lord hath set apart him that is godly for Himself."* You see, the *"for Himself"* hinges upon the *"set apart."* **There is no consecration without separation.** If you are mourning over want of realized consecration, will you look humbly and sincerely into this point? *"A garden enclosed is my sister, my spouse,"* saith the Heavenly Bridegroom.

> *Set a part for Jesus!*
> *Is not this enough,*
> *Though the desert prospect*
> *Open wild and rough?*
> *Set apart for His delight,*
> *Chosen for His Holy pleasure,*
> *Sealed to be His special treasure!*
> *Could we choose a nobler joy?*
> *— And would we, if we might?*

But yielding, by His grace, to this blessed setting apart for Himself, "The Lord shall <u>establish</u> thee an Holy people unto Himself, as He hath sworn unto thee." Can there be a stronger promise? Just obey and trust His word *now*, and yield yourselves *now* unto God, *"that He may establish thee <u>to-day</u> for a people unto Himself."* Commit the keeping of your souls to Him in well-doing, as unto a faithful Creator, being persuaded that He is **ABLE TO KEEP** that which you commit to Him.

Now, Lord, I give myself to Thee,
I would be wholly Thine,
As Thou hast given Thyself to me,
And Thou art wholly mine;
O take me, seal me for Thine own,
Thine altogether, Thine alone.

Here comes in once more that immeasurably important subject of our influence. **For it is not what we say or do, so much as what we are, that influences others.** We have heard this, and very likely repeated it again and again, but have we seen it to be inevitably linked with the great question of this chapter? *I do not know anything which, thoughtfully considered, makes us realize more vividly the need and the importance of our whole selves being kept for Jesus.* Any part not wholly committed, and not wholly kept, must hinder and neutralize the real influence for Him of all the rest. If we ourselves are kept all for Jesus, then our influence will be all kept for Him too. If not, then, however much we may wish and talk and try, we cannot throw our full weight into the right scale. And just in so far as it is not in the one scale, it must be in the other; weighing against the little which we have tried to put in the right one and making the short weight still shorter.

So large a proportion of it is entirely involuntary, while yet the responsibility of it is so enormous, that our helplessness comes out in exceptionally strong relief, while our past debt in this matter is simply incalculable. Are we feeling this a little? Getting just a glimpse, down the misty passages of memory, of the neutral influence, the wasted influence, the mistaken influence, the actually wrong influence which has marked the ineffaceable although untraceable course? And all the while we owed Him all that influence! It *ought* to have been all for Him! We have nothing to say. But what has our Lord to say? *"I forgave thee all <u>that</u> debt!"*

Then, after that forgiveness which must come first, there comes a thought of great comfort in our freshly felt helplessness, rising out of the very thing that makes us realize this helplessness. Just because our influence is to such a great extent involuntary and unconscious, we may rest assured that if we ourselves are truly kept for Jesus, this will be, as a quite natural result, kept for Him also. It cannot be otherwise, for as is the fountain, so will be the flow; as. the spring, so the action; as the impulse, so the communicated motion. Thus there may be, and in simple trust there will be, a quiet rest about it, a relief from all sense of strain and effort, a fulfilling of the words, *"For he that is entered into his rest, he also hath ceased from his own works, as God did from His."* It will not be a matter of *trying* to have good influence, but just of *having* it, as naturally and constantly as the magnetized bar.

Another encouraging thought should follow. Of ourselves we may have but little weight, no particular talents or position or anything else to put into the scale; but let us remember that again and again God has shown that the influence of a very average life, when once really consecrated to Him, may outweigh that of almost any number of merely professing Christians. Such lives are like Gideon's three hundred, carrying not even the ordinary weapons of war, but only trumpets and lamps and empty pitchers, by whom the Lord wrought great deliverance, while He did not use the others at all. For He hath chosen the weak things of the world to confound the things which are mighty.

Should not all this be additional motive for desiring that our *whole* selves should be taken and *kept?* I know that *"whatsoever God doeth, it shall be forever"*. Therefore, we may rejoicingly say *"ever"* as well as *"only"* and *"all for Thee!"* For the Lord is our Keeper, and He is the Almighty and the Everlasting God, with *"whom is no variableness, neither shadow of turning"*. He will never change His mind about keeping us, and no man is able to pluck us out of His hand. Neither will Christ let us pluck ourselves out of His hand, for He says, *"Thou shall abide for Me many days."* And He that keepeth us will not slumber. Once having undertaken His vineyard, He will keep it night and day, till all the days and nights are over, and we know the full meaning of the salvation ready to be revealed in the last time, unto which we are kept by His power.

And then, forever for Him! ...Passing from the gracious keeping by faith for this little while, to the glorious keeping in His presence for all eternity! ...Forever fulfilling the object for which He formed us and chose us — we showing forth His praise and He showing the exceeding riches of His grace in His kindness towards us in the ages to come! *He for us, and we for Him forever....* Oh, how little we can grasp this! Yet this is the fruition of being *"kept for Jesus!"*

Pondering Points
BY KATIE GARRAWAY

The needful truth has returned to us again regarding a life that is truly consecrated unto Christ. However, it has been taken a step further. The point was emphasized that there can be no true Biblical consecration without Biblical separation. We must be willing to turn our back on the flesh, the world, sin, and any carnal practice that would hinder us from living in complete surrender.

Pastor / Evangelist J. Wilber Chapman determined, "Anything that dims my vision of Christ, or takes away my love for Him — or removes my taste for Bible study, or cramps my prayer life, or makes Christian work difficult, is wrong for me, and I must turn away from it!" And with this mindset, God used him mightily in reaching and training a generation for Christ.

*If there is one thing in churches under attack today more than anything else, it is the doctrine of separation. Many are compromising from the certain truths of Scripture, claiming the "age of grace" to justify their carnal practices and acceptance of worldly influences. But God's grace does not blur the lines and blend everything together. It proclaims disctinction. "For the grace of God that bringeth salvation hath appeared to all men, Teaching us that, **denying** ungodliness and worldly lusts, <u>we should live soberly, righteously, and godly</u>, in this present world; Looking for that blessed hope, and the glorious appearing of the great God and our Saviour Jesus Christ; Who gave himself for us, that he might redeem us from all iniquity, and <u>purify **unto himself** a peculiar people</u>, zealous of good works" (Titus 2:11-14).*

Yes, God's grace brings us wonderful freedom and liberty! However, it does not give us freedom <u>to</u> sin but freedom <u>from</u> sin (Romans 6:1-2). It does not give us liberty from Christ but liberty in Christ. Grace is there to teach us how to live like our precious Saviour, and it has never been given to provide license for us to live like a perverse sinner.

Christ desires for us and demands of us to be actively engaged in separation and holy living. "Be ye holy, for I am holy" (I Peter 1:16). "Wherefore come out from among them, and be ye separate, saith the Lord, and touch not the unclean thing; and I will receive you" (II Corinthians 6:17). *His position and precepts on this has never changed — "with whom is no variableness, neither shadow of turning"* (James 1:17).

Do you see a personal need for Biblical separation in your life? Do you struggle with accepting this? Are you willing to live a separated life in any way the Lord leads you according to His Word? Is there anything in the Bible that you are not willing to apply to your life in the area of separation? Have you made personal commitments through Biblical conviction to be separate from the world and carnal things? Or are you seeking to use your liberty in Christ to justify any secular practices?

In what ways has God led you, developed you, grown you, and strengthened you in this over the years? Or have you allowed your life to grow weak in its passion for Biblical separation? Did you use to have healthy Biblical standards 2 or 3 years ago that you have now dropped? "Therefore we ought to give the more earnest heed to the things which we have heard, lest at any time we should let them slip." (Hebrews 2:1). *Do you find yourself with less of a passion and awareness for holiness now than where you were in your relationship with Christ at some point in your past? Did someone influence you to make this decision? If so, why?*

Do you realize that through your testimony and what you do, what you wear, what you say, what activities you engage in, and how you handle yourself — it is affecting and influencing others around you? Are you striving to govern yourself with doctrine, dignity, discernment, and distinction? Are you willing to separate from anything unto Christ if He directed you to do so? What are you saying "No" to so that you may gladly say "Yes" even more passionately to Christ?

These are all such very important questions to pray through and ponder. *"But evil men and seducers shall wax worse and worse, deceiving, and being deceived. But continue thou in the things which thou hast learned and hast been assured of, knowing of whom thou hast learned them; And that from a child thou hast known the holy scriptures, which are able to make thee wise unto salvation through faith which is in Christ Jesus. All scripture is given by inspiration of God, and is profitable for doctrine, for reproof, for correction, for instruction in righteousness: That the man of God may be perfect, throughly furnished unto all good works."* (II Timothy 3:13-17).

CHAPTER 13
Christ For Us!

"So will I also be for Thee." — Hosea 3:3

The typical promise, *"Thou shalt abide for Me many days,"* is indeed a marvel of love. For it is given to the most undeserving, described under the strongest possible figure of utter worthlessness and treacherousness — the woman beloved, yet an adulteress.

The depth of the abyss shows the length of the line that has fathomed it, yet only the length of the line reveals the real depth of the abyss. The sin shows the love, and the love reveals the sin. The Bible has few words more touching, though seldom quoted, than those just preceding this wonderful promise: *"The love of the Lord toward the children of Israel, who look to other gods, and love flagons of wine."* Put that into the personal application which no doubt underlies it, and say, *"The love of the Lord toward <u>me</u>, who have looked away from Him, with wandering, faithless eyes, to other helps and hopes, and have loved earthly joys and sought earthly gratifications — the love of the Lord toward even <u>me</u>!"* And then hear Him saying in the next verse,

"*So I bought her to Me;*" stooping to do that in His unspeakable condescension of love, not with the typical silver and barley, but with the precious blood of Christ Then, having thus loved us, and rescued us, and bought us with a price indeed, He says, still under the same figure, "*Thou shalt abide for Me many days.*"

This is both a command and a pledge. But the very pledge implies our past unfaithfulness, and the proved need of even our own part being undertaken by the ever patient Lord. He Himself has to guarantee our faithfulness, because there is no other hope of our continuing faithful. Well may such love win our full and glad surrender, and such a promise win our happy and confident trust!

But He says more. He says, "*So will I also be for thee!*" And this seems an even greater marvel of love, as we observe how He meets every detail of our consecration with this wonderful word.

HIS LIFE FOR THEE. "*The Good Shepherd giveth His life for the sheep.*" Oh, wonderful gift! not promised, but given; not to friends, but to enemies. Given without condition, without reserve, without return. Himself unknown and unloved, His gift unsought and unasked, He gave His life for thee; a more than royal bounty — the greatest gift that Deity could devise. Oh, grandeur of love! "*I lay down My life for the sheep!*" And we for whom He gave it have held back, and hesitated to give our lives, not even far Him (He has not asked us to do that), but to Him! But that is past, and He has tenderly pardoned the unloving, ungrateful reserve, and has graciously accepted the poor little fleeting breath and speck of dust which was all we had to offer. And now His precious death and glorious life are all "*for thee.*"

HIS ETERNITY FOR THEE. All we can ask Him to take are days and moments — the little span given us as it is given, and of this only the present in deed and the future in will. As for the past, in so far as we did not give it to Him, it is too late; we can never give it now! But His past was given to us, though ours was not given to Him. Oh, what a tremendous debt does this show us! Away back in the dim depths of past eternity, *"or ever the earth and the world were made,"* His divine existence in the bosom of His Father was all *"for thee,"* purposing and planning *"for thee,"* receiving and holding the promise of eternal life *"for thee."*

Then the thirty-three years among sinners on this sinful earth: do we think enough of the slowly-wearing days and nights, the heavy-footed hours, the never-hastening minutes, that went to make up those thirty- three years of trial and humiliation? We all know how slowly time passes when suffering and sorrow are near, and there is no reason to suppose that our Master was exempted from this part of our infirmities.

Then His present is *"for thee."* Even now He *"liveth to make intercession;"* even now He *"thinketh upon me;"* even now He *"knoweth,"* He *"careth,"* He *"loveth."*

Then, only to think that His whole eternity will be *"for thee!"* Millions of ages of unfoldings of all His love, and of ever new declarings of His Father's name to His brethren. Think of it! and can we ever hesitate to give all our poor little hours to His service?

HIS HANDS FOR THEE. Literal hands; literally pierced, when the whole weight of His quivering frame hung from their torn muscles and bared nerves; literally uplifted in parting blessing. Consecrated, priestly hands; *"filled"* hands (Exodus 28:41, 29:9, etc.) — filled once with His great offering, and now with gifts and blessings *"for thee."* Tender hands, touching and healing, lifting and leading with gentlest care. Strong hands, upholding and defending. Open hands, filling with good and satisfying desire (Psalm 104:28 & 145:16). Faithful hands, restraining and sustaining. *"His left hand is under my head, and His right hand doth embrace me."*

HIS FEET FOR THEE. They were weary very often, they were wounded and bleeding once. They made clear footprints as He went about doing good, and as He went up to Jerusalem to suffer; and these *"blessed steps of His most Holy life,"* both as substitution and example, were *"for thee."* Our place of waiting and learning, of resting and loving, is at His feet. And still those *"blessed feet"* are and shall be *"for thee,"* until He comes again to receive us unto Himself, until and when the word is fulfilled, *"They shall walk with Me in white."*

HIS VOICE FOR THEE. The *"voice of my beloved that knocketh, saying, Open to me, my sister, my love;"* the voice that His sheep *"hear"* and *"know,"* and that calls out the fervent response, *"Master, say on!"* This is not all. It was the literal voice of the Lord Jesus which uttered that one echoless cry of desolation on the Cross for thee, and it will be His own literal voice which will say, *"Come, ye blessed!"* to thee. And that same tender and glorious voice has literally sung and will sing for thee. I think He consecrated song for us, and made it a sweet and sacred thing for ever, when He Himself *"sang an hymn,"* the very last thing before He went forth to consecrate suffering for us. That was not His last song. *"The Lord thy God . . . will joy over thee with singing."* And the time is coming when He will not only sing *"for thee"* or *"over thee,"* but *"with thee"*! He says He will! *"In the midst of the church will I sing praise unto Thee."* Now what a magnificent glimpse of joy this is! *"Jesus Himself leading* *the praises of His brethren,"* and we ourselves singing not merely in such a chorus, but with such a leader! If singing for Jesus is such delight here, what will this singing *with* Jesus be? Surely song may well be a Holy thing to us henceforth.

HIS LIPS FOR THEE. Perhaps there is no part of our consecration which it is so difficult practically to realize, and in which it is, therefore, so needful to recollect — *"I also for thee."* It is often helpful to read straight through one or more of the Gospels with a special thought —*"His lips for me!"* — on our mind and see how much bears upon it. When we read one through with this thought wondering, verse by verse, at the grace which was poured into them, and the gracious words which fell from them, wondering more and more at the cumulative force and infinite wealth of tenderness and power and wisdom and love flowing from them, we cannot but desire that our lips and all the fruit of them should be wholly for Him. *"For thee"* they were opened in blessing; *"for thee"* they were closed when He was led as a lamb to the slaughter. And whether teaching, warning, counsel, comfort, or encouragement, commandments in whose keeping there is a great reward, or promises which exceed all we ask or think-all the precious fruit of His lips is *"for thee,"* really and truly meant *"for thee."*

HIS WEALTH FOR THEE. *"Though He was rich, yet for our sakes He became, poor, that ye through His poverty might be made rich."* Yes, through His poverty the unsearchable riches of Christ are "for thee." Seven-fold riches are mentioned; and these are no unminted treasure or sealed reserve, but all ready coined for our use, and stamped with His own image and superscription, and poured freely into the hand of faith. The mere list is wonderful. *"Riches of goodness," "riches of* *forbearance and long-suffering,*" "*riches both of wisdom and knowledge,*" "*riches of mercy,*" "*exceeding riches of grace,*" and "*riches of glory.*" And His own Word says, "*All are yours!*" Glance on in faith, and think of eternity flowing on and on beyond the mightiest sweep of imagination, and realize that all "*His riches in glory*" and "*the riches of His glory*" are and shall be "*for thee!*" In view of this, shall we care to reserve anything that rust doth corrupt for ourselves?

HIS TREASURES OF "WISDOM AND KNOWLEDGE" FOR THEE. First, used for our behalf and benefit Why did He expend such immeasurable might of mind upon a world which is to be burnt up, but that He would fit it perfectly to be, not the home, but the school of His children? The infinity of His skill is such that the most powerful intellects find a lifetime too short to penetrate a little way into a few secrets of some one small department of His working. If we turn to Providence, it is quite enough to take only one's own life, and look at it microscopically and telescopically, and marvel at the treasures of wisdom lavished upon its details, ordering and shaping and fitting the tiny confused bits into the true mosaic which He means it to be. Many a little thing in our lives reveals the same Mind which, according to a well-known and very beautiful illustration, adjusted a perfect proportion in the delicate hinges of the snowdrop and the droop of its bell, with the mass of the globe and the force of gravitation. How kind we think it if a very talented friend spends a little of his thought and power of mind in teaching us or planning for us! Have we been grateful for the infinite thought and wisdom which our Lord has expended upon us and our creation, preservation, and redemption?

Secondly, to be shared with us. He says, *"All that I have is thine."* He holds nothing back, reserves nothing from His dear children, and what we cannot receive now He is keeping for us. He gives us *"hidden riches of secret places"* now, but by and by He will give us more, and the glorified intellect will be filled continually out of His treasures of wisdom and knowledge. But the sanctified intellect will be, must be, used for Him, and only for Him, now!

HIS WILL FOR THEE. Think first of the *infinite might* of that will; the first great law and the first great force of the universe, from which alone every other law and every other force has sprung, and to which all are subordinate. *"He worketh all things after the counsel of His own will." "He doeth according to His will in the army of heaven, and among the inhabitants of the earth."* Then think of the infinite mysteries of that will. For ages and generations, the hosts of heaven have wonderingly watched its vouchsafed unveilings and its sublime developments, and still they are waiting, watching, and wondering.

Creation and Providence are but the whisper of its power, but Redemption is its music, and praise is the echo which shall yet fill His temple. The whisper and the music, yes, and *"the thunder of His power,"* are all *"for thee."* For what *is* *"the good pleasure of His will"*? (Ephesians 1:5) Oh, what a grand list of blessings purposed, provided, purchased, and possessed, all flowing to us out of it! And nothing but blessings, nothing but privileges, which we never should have imagined, and which, even when revealed, we are *"slow of heart to believe;"* nothing but what should even now fill us *"with joy unspeakable and full of glory!"*

Think of this will as always and altogether on our side — always working for us, and in us, and with us, if we will only let it; think of it as always and only synonymous with infinitely wise and almighty love. Think of it as undertaking all for us, from the great work of our eternal salvation down to the momentary details of guidance and supply. And do we not feel utter shame and self-abhorrence at *ever* having hesitated for an instant to give up our tiny, feeble, blind will, to be — not crushed, not even bent, — but *blended* with His glorious and perfect Will?

HIS HEART FOR THEE. *"Behold . . . He is mighty . . . in heart"* (Job 36:5). And this mighty and tender heart is *"for thee!"* If He had only stretched forth His hand to save us from bare destruction, and said, *"My hand for thee!"* how could we have praised Him enough? But what shall we say of the unspeakably marvellous condescension which says, *"Thou hast ravished my heart, my sister, my spouse!"* The very fountain of His divine life, and light, and love, the very centre of His being, is given to His beloved ones, who are not only *"set as a seal upon His heart,"* but taken into His heart, so that our life is hid there, and we dwell there in the very centre of all safety, and power, and love, and glory. What will be the revelation of that day, when the Lord Jesus promises, *"Ye shall know that I am in My Father, and ye in Me"*? For He implies that we do not yet know it, and that our present knowledge of this dwelling in Him is not knowledge at all compared with what He is going to show us about it. Now shall we, can we, reserve any corner of our hearts from Him?

HIS LOVE FOR THEE. Not a passive, possible love, but outflowing, yes, *outpouring* of the real, glowing, personal love of His mighty and tender heart Love not as an attribute, a quality, a latent force, but an acting, moving, reaching, touching, and grasping power. Love, not a cold, beautiful, far-off star, but a sunshine that comes and enfolds us, making us warm and glad, and strong and bright and fruitful.

His love! What manner of love is it? What should be quoted to prove or describe it? First the whole Bible with its mysteries and marvels of redemption, then the whole book of Providence and the whole volume of creation. Then add to these the unknown records of eternity past and the unknown glories of eternity to come, and then let the immeasurable quotation be sung by *"angels and archangels, and all the company of heaven,"* with all the harps of God, and still that love will be untold, still it will be *"the love of Christ that passeth knowledge."*

But it is completely *"for thee!"*

HIMSELF FOR THEE. *"Christ also hath loved us, and given Himself for us." "The Son of God . . . loved me, and gave Himself for me."* Yes, Himself! What is the Bride's true and central treasure? What calls forth the deepest, brightest, sweetest thrill of love and praise? Not the Bridegroom's priceless gifts, not the robe of His resplendent righteousness, not the dowry of unsearchable riches, not the magnificence of the palace home to which He is bringing her, not the glory which she shall share with Him, but HIMSELF! Jesus Christ, *"who His own self bare our sins in His own body on the tree;" "this same Jesus," "whom having not seen, ye love;"* the Son of God, and the Man of Sorrows; my Saviour, my Friend, my Master, my King, my Priest, my Lord and my God — HE says, *"I also for thee!"* What an *"I"!* What power and sweetness we feel in it, so different from any human *"I,"* for all His Godhead and all His manhood are concentrated in it, and all *"for thee!"*

And not only *"all"* but *"ever"* for thee! His unchangeableness is the seal upon every attribute; He will be *"this same Jesus"* forever. How can mortal mind estimate this enormous promise? How can mortal heart conceive what is enfolded in these words, *"I also for thee"*?

One glimpse of its fulness and glory, and we feel that henceforth it must be, shall be, and by His grace will be our true-hearted, whole-hearted cry —

Take myself, and I will be
Ever, ONLY, ALL for Thee!

Pondering Points
BY KATIE GARRAWAY

May the faithfulness, goodness, and love of our Savior wash over us anew as we behold Him in all His glory! Do you allow your heart to be continually overwhelmed with the wonder of Christ day by day? Or has the wonder "worn off"? Many times in revival history, when a church had lost this right perspective and then through deep conviction saw Him afresh for Who He truly was, they experienced a great work of Heaven in their midst. During the First Great Awakening, Jonathan Edwards wrote of what he witnessed: "Several personas have had so great a sense of the glory of God, and excellence of Christ, that nature and life seemed almost to sink under it; and in all probability, if God had showed them a little more of Himself, it would have dissolved their frame. A true sense of the glorious excellence of the Lord Jesus Christ, and of His wonderful dying love, and the exercise of a truly spiritual love [unto Him], should…very much…overcome the bodily strength."

We must beware of the danger of losing our awe with God through familiarity. If we're not careful, His miracles can become a mere series of facts in history. Our daily relationship with Him will become common because it's customary routine - always reading / always attending / always doing. Robotic. Lifeless. Thoughtless motions. Our service unto God will deteriorate into joyless obligation.

The fact is we lose our awe with Christ if something or someone else becomes <u>more</u> fascinating to us. Have we become bored with God? Have we forgotten that His mercies are new every morning, His compassions fail not, His faithfulness is great, His grace is sufficient, His power is limitless, and His love is inseparable? Have we have become so infatuated with earthly, temporal things that are so incomparable to His eternal riches? May we experience the realness of God with every fiber of our being! His glory should make our heart swell. His person and presence should rule every domain of our existence! At the end of the day, ask yourself who and what you are saying "Wow" to? And who and what are others saying "Wow" to because of you? May Jesus ever and always enrapture our hearts!

CONCLUSION
— by Katie Garraway —

What a journey of consecration this has been! Does your heart, mind, and life feel refreshed and strengthened by the exhortation, encouragement, and conviction the Lord has tenderly brought to us through these powerful reflections? Certainly, the familiar lines of Frances Havergal's sacred hymn, **"Take My Life and Let It Be"**, hold a richer and fuller meaning. We have probably sung this song hundreds of times in our lives — in a church service, a youth rally, a camp meeting, a revival or conference — not even fully comprehending the depth of the messages of each line, the passion behind every phrase written. No longer will they be mere words we learned as a child growing up in church or lyrics on a hymnal's page! They will now deep-seated statements of personal dedication unto our great Saviour Who has given us all things.

Have you taken the time, at the end of each chapter, to ponder, meditate, commune with God and surrender each area of your life over to Him? Was there any part that you rushed past and now feel guilty over, knowing you have held it back and are not willing to lay it at His feet? Why not stop right now and speak with your Heavenly Father about it. Experience the joy and relief that can flood your heart when you know you have fully surrendered your all to Him!

And the next time you sing this soul-stirring hymn as a congregational in your church service or hear it played during the invitation, don't just mumble the words without much thought to the meaning behind what you're singing. May each line remind you of the chapters you read here, and the decisions you've made — the areas you surrendered. Sing with passion as you re-declare your ALL unto Him, and triumphantly rejoice in the great privilege we have in daily consecrating our everything for the Master's use!

ABOUT THE COMPILER

Katie Garraway was born on November 9, 1985, and was blessed to be able to grow up in a Christian home as a Pastor's daughter. She accepted the Lord as her Savior in 1991 and surrendered her life to the Lord's work in 1997. When she was a teenager, God began to burden her heart to be an evangelist's wife. Through the years, God has allowed Katie to use her musical gifts in the local church as pianist, singer, children's choir director, and teacher. She has written several songs and has recorded multiple albums with her husband Caleb.

Caleb and Katie were married on March 20, 2010. They travel in full-time evangelism a majority of each year with hearts that burn for Heaven-sent revival. Their ministries have reached scores of millions globally with the Gospel through preaching, the printed word, music, and film. They offer many other resources (music albums, documentaries, and books) for the church, family, and home.

Katie has written several books including *Let God Write Your Love Story, Modesty: An Issue of the Heart, Thriving As A Busy Mom,* and has co-authored three books with her husband Caleb — *A Biblical Approach to Music, The Secret of the Lost Scrolls,* and *The Legend of the Immortal Kingdom.*

Caleb and Katie have been blessed with five precious children and always enjoy spending time at their home in Washington, IA, when their schedule will allow. Please visit *www.remnantministriesonline.com* for more details.